REMINGTON HANDGUNS

ELIPHALET REMINGTON

REMINGTON HANDGUNS

CHARLES LEE KARR, JR.

And

CAROLL ROBBINS KARR

BONANZA BOOKS · NEW YORK

Acknowledgments

We wish to acknowledge our great indebtedness to Mr. C. C. Loomis, of the Design Section of the Remington Ilion plant. Mr. Loomis possesses invaluable data which, but for his personal interest in the company's history and his efforts over the years to gather and preserve information, might have been forever lost. He gave generously of material on the little known or heretofore unknown handgun models and even more generously of his time. His wide knowledge of Remington history was the background of many interesting and rewarding hours of conversation.

We appreciate the kindness of Mr. Rutherford and of others at the Ilion plant, whose patience must have been tried by our interruptions in these hectic times.

To Mr. J. M. K. Abbott, Manager of Public Relations, we are indebted for arranging visits to the Ilion and Bridgeport plants and for providing background material. His interest and aid were of no small value.

Lt. Colonel Calvin Goddard, U.S.A., has given constant assistance and encouragement. He not only lent material from his personal library but helped locate source material elsewhere. His suggestions and advice have been invaluable.

Special thanks are due Mr. John Hintlian, of Newington, Connecticut, who granted us the use of his extensive firearms library and also lent us valuable books and catalogs for extended periods.

The technical skill and counsel of Mr. Howard Moore, photographer of Ilion, relieved us of a considerable burden. The clarity and detail of his pictures speak for themselves.

We are grateful to Mr. Roger C. Peterson, of Portland, Maine, and Mr. Jonathan Peck, of Hartford, Connecticut, who sent guns from their collections to Mr. Moore to be photographed; to the Girard Chambers, Junior and Senior, who arranged for photographs of three Remingtons in their collection; and to Mr. Claude Fuller, of Chattanooga, Tennessee, for the use of a volume in his library. Mr. Ray Riling, of Philadelphia, provided the data on Remington pistol flasks.

CONTENTS

FOREWORD

This little volume represents one more foundation stone in the edifice which is the story of the Handgun in America. It is a sturdy block, carefully hewn and polished, and the two workmen who quarried and laid it have produced a job which is plumb, square, and level. Let us hope that it represents but the first of many such contributions which they will make to the structure which has been so long a-building, and of which so much remains to be completed.

True, we have the stories of Colt, of Smith and Wesson, and of American military sidearms. But how many are yet lacking! In the cartridge period alone a quick review brings forth the names of Marlin, Stevens, Hopkins and Allen, Thames, Warner, Forehand and Wadsworth, Ethan Allen, Allen and Wheelock, Fyrberg (and the myriad brands produced under his patents in the Sears-Roebuck plant at Meriden, Conn.), Otis A. Smith, American Arms Co., Wesson and Harrington, Reid and his "Knuckle-Dusters," the Chicago Arms Co. and the Minneapolis Arms Co. "Squeezers," Shattuck and his four-barrelled palm pistol (and revolvers as well), and scores of others. None of these with the possible exception of Stevens is now producing hand arms and with each day that passes the source material from which their histories must be put together becomes more difficult of access. And when we cast back to the percussion era, with its unnumbered types and makers, the difficulties increase a thousand fold. Of the flint period so little documentation remains that once we leave the field of military types the task becomes well-nigh impossible. Fortunately, however, at least from the historian's standpoint, few handguns of significance were then being produced in this country for other than the military, so we are not so badly off as might at first appear.

The authors of *Remington Handguns* possess a unique combination of qualifications. Commander Karr is an engineer and goes at his work with the exactness peculiar to that calling. His wife is experienced in historical research, and both have versatile pens. Lastly, both *like* to shoot—and *can* shoot. As a result they now have presented us a finished product which combines accuracy, completeness of coverage, and high readability. Having in my time waded through, as a book reviewer, some thousands of pages of "gun books" contrived by individuals whose only claim to fame lay in their ability to shoot a weapon accurately (having yet to make the most casual acquaintance with even the rudiments of the King's English), or who had done writing of a sort in other pastures and were now breaking into the arms field because it appeared to offer a rich harvest, it is a refreshing experience to meet a work such as this. Would that I might more often indulge in such a treat!

Calvin Goddard

Preface to First Edition

This book grew out of the difficulties we encountered in our search for information on the Remington handguns. Little had been presented on these arms; and that little was widely scattered, generally inaccurate, and often in a form unavailable to the average collector. Our first idea was to compile a catalog giving complete and accurate descriptions and illustrations of every model of Remington handgun, together with a brief history of the Remington Company. The response of collector friends impressed upon us the real need for information on the Remington pistols and revolvers, the even more eager desire for the whole Remington story. So almost at once, the catalog became a book.

The volume was written primarily for the collector. The original catalog has been preserved intact and separate from the "story" sections for quick and easy reference. Chapter Eight, "Notes for the Shooter," was included not so much for the cap-and-ball enthusiast, who has already discovered the merits of the old Remingtons and needs no directions for shooting them, but for the collector who might wish to join the ever growing number of muzzle-loaders, or simply to try one of his Remingtons. Chapter Seven, "Notes for the Collector," was designed with the newcomer —to the collecting hobby or to the Remington handguns—in mind, but will, perhaps, answer some of the questions "oldtimers" have asked us.

We hope that this volume, as well as meeting the wants of collectors, will do justice to the well worth telling and long over-due story of the Remington handguns and the men of imagination, inventive genius, and enterprise who produced them.

Charles and Caroll Karr.

Indian Orchard, Mass.

Preface to Second Edition

During the five years since we finished our original manuscript, we have collected and shot and traded and looked at a great many more Remingtons. And we have, of course, always continued our search for information about these arms and their makers.

While in Seattle, Washington, in 1947, we had the great good fortune to meet Mrs. Fred Remington Greene, widow of Philo Remington's grandson. As a young bride, visiting her husband's grandparents, she could not hear too often the stories of great-grandfather Eliphalet or too much about the early days of his business and the later adventures of his enterprising sons. We in turn could not hear enough—and treasure the hours Mrs. Greene so graciously gave us.

We were able to examine the family collection of firearms then in Mrs. Greene's possession and to purchase it after her death. The particular arms most treasured by Philo and his grandson were the handguns, mounted in a case that had stood originally in the firm's New York showroom. With but few exceptions, these were presentation pieces illustrating the special grips, plating and engraving done by the Remington Company.

Many of you have written us of Remington handguns in your possession. Your letters—surely one of the most satisfying of rewards for our effort—have added interesting and illuminating details to the handgun story.

Judging from your letters, and comments when we meet, you would very much like to know more about the special arms—such as inventor's models—and the variations from standard in mechanical detail or fittings. So this revision will serve as a "clearing house" of comment on the unusual.

You have often asked for more about the Remington Company, the family and the legends told of them. This, the handgun story, is not the proper place, we feel. The first Remington was a rifle, and through one hundred and thirty-five years now Remington has continued to make rifles. Handguns were produced in volume only during a brief thirty-year period of this long history. And so now, as before, we leave much for another story.

Avon, Connecticut   Charles and Caroll Karr.

1 ▪ ▪

The Story of the
Remington Arms

EARLY IN 1816, Eliphalet Remington, of Ilion, New York, decided to make his own rifle and produced the first Remington arm, a muzzle-loading flintlock. He forged the barrel from scrap iron, then walked fifteen miles to Utica to have it rifled. Morgan James, the gunsmith who did the rifling, was so impressed that he gave young Remington the lock. Eliphalet returned to Ilion, shaped a stock to his liking, and completed the gun. It was good—good enough to create an immediate demand for others like it. So began the Remington gun business.

According to tradition, Eliphalet's decision to make a rifle stemmed from his father's refusal to buy him one. An interest in things mechanical and a desire to "see what he could do" are more likely reasons for his determination. The making of the rifle was not the first evidence of this bent of mind. Sent, as a young boy, to the silversmith in Herkimer to have silver dollars made into spoons, Eliphalet watched the silversmith work, returned with the dollars, and made the spoons himself. Eliphalet's father, carpenter and mechanic as well as successful farmer, recognized and encouraged his son's ability. The senior Remington, who had migrated to New York state from Connecticut in 1800, installed a forge on that part of his farm known as Ilion Gulph, where Steele's creek provided the necessary water power. There, father and son had carried on a substantial business, making farm implements and doing general repair work for farmers, for some years before the younger Remington made his first rifle. There, filling the neighbors' orders for similar guns, Eliphalet launched the Remington arms industry.

The making of guns rapidly became the most important business at the forge. At first, Eliphalet had the barrels rifled by Morgan James. Walking the thirty miles to Utica and back, he delivered a new batch to the gunsmith and returned with the lot left on the preceding trip. But before long he contrived a rifling machine of his own. He soon devised and installed other machinery for finishing the interior and exterior of barrels. Grindstones to smooth the welded edges of barrels were quarried from a red sandstone ledge nearby. As Remington's reputation as a fine arms maker grew and spread, he began manufacturing pistol and rifle barrels for gunsmiths and hardware merchants as well as completed guns for his own customer list. Shipments went by stagecoach, then by canal. By 1828 the gun business had outgrown the forge: constantly expanding trade and ever larger shipments necessitated improved transportation facilities. The Remingtons purchased land in Ilion proper, built a shop on the canal, and installed the machinery taken from the forge. The elder Remington died in 1828 as the result of an accident which occurred during the building of that shop.

Within a year Eliphalet found even the new establishment inadequate. He constructed another building, the "Stone Forge," to meet the demand for gun barrels. That same year, 1829, he set up a shipping department stocked with gun parts and accessories. He started to work then on a system of interchangeable parts. He had already begun experimenting with materials. In the earlier years, Eliphalet had sent teams about the countryside for scrap iron. Later he secured iron ore from the Clinton ore beds in Oneida county. By 1829 he had tried steel in gun barrels. In the early forge fires he used charcoal burned from timber cut around Ilion. In 1829 he experimented with coal. The shop and forge took on the character of a modern plant.

At the plant on the canal as in the earlier forge in the gulph Eliphalet constantly invented, improvised, and improved machinery, methods, and materials. He never hesitated at change if change might mean betterment. Nor did he ever refuse to listen to a new idea. His interest in inventors and his willingness to hear them out attracted to Ilion men with ideas of every description in every stage of development. To the plant on the canal came inventors with models, inventors with sketches, inventors with just theories. Many of those who came and much of the work they did had no direct connection with the gun business. But the inventive spirit which pervaded every Remington enterprise guided the development of Remington arms.

In 1845 the factory started work on the first Remington service arms—the first standard models manufactured in great numbers. Before that time Remington rifles, shotguns, and pistols were almost entirely custom guns, altered constantly to incorporate new ideas. Although Remington continued to do custom gunsmithing, the majority of Remington arms after 1845 were standard models. In that year the firm took over a government contract for 5,000 rifles of the Harpers Ferry pattern from a John Griffiths, of Cincinnati, Ohio, and shortly afterward a government contract for Jencks carbines from N. P. Ames, of Springfield, Massachusetts. Eliphalet added another building, the "Old Armory," and constructed the "upper" water race. Even before he completed the original contracts, additional orders came.

In 1856 Philo, Samuel, and Eliphalet, Jr. became partners of their father in the firm of E. Remington and Sons. Philo, the eldest, born in 1816, had mastered every branch of the technical work. He was as competent a gun maker as his father, and like him, equally competent at directing the work of others. Samuel, two years younger, had previously engaged in separate ventures of his own. After an unsuccessful try at railroad construction in the West, he returned to Ilion where he manufactured brooms, then Yale locks, bank vault doors, and, in 1855, two hundred breech-loading guns under Merrill's patent. Samuel dropped these separate endeavors when he entered the partnership. Eliphalet, Jr., the youngest, born in 1828, had, like Philo, remained with his

From the family estate

PLATE I. AN OLD REMINGTON CIRCULAR.

father, but in the office rather than the plant work. The establishment of the firm was an outward symbol of rapid growth and development in the "50's." A brochure put out the following year, 1857, announced the manufacture of a "New and Superior Revolver," the first of the Remington percussion revolvers.

When the threatened Civil War became tragic actuality in 1861, Remington turned its energies and equipment to producing arms for the Government. The company added new buildings, purchased new tools and machinery, and installed steam power. Even with this expansion, the "Armory" could not meet the government orders that poured in. To fill the contracts for service revolvers, the firm rented a building in Utica and equipped it with additional tools and machinery. The entire organization worked day and night, and no one harder than its founder and head. The tremendous strain was too great: Eliphalet Remington died on August 12, 1861. Philo took over management of the manufacturing department; Samuel became contract negotiator and purchasing agent; Eliphalet, Jr. assumed direction of the office and correspondence. In 1865 a corporation keeping the name "E. Remington and Sons" succeeded the partnership.

In April of 1865 the company faced a serious crisis. Abrupt termination of all government purchases of arms immediately the Civil War ended brought production to a sudden halt. Remington had incurred considerable indebtedness in the rapid expansion necessary to produce arms needed by the Government during the war. The company had flatly refused to join in the wartime profiteering so common during the emergency; in fact, their contract prices were so low that the firm now found itself in critical financial straits. Remington had already developed a new breech-loading arm. Securing extension of notes and new credits, the firm set to work to perfect it and to "re-tool" the plant for its manufacture. With the success of this famous "rolling-block" action breech-loader, the company again prospered. The Remingtons paid in full with interest the claims of all stockholders and depositors of the Ilion Bank which had closed in the crisis.

The years that followed brought ever increased activity and fame to the Remingtons and Ilion. Experiment and improvement produced new guns and improved models. In 1866 Remington advertised revolvers, rifles, muskets and carbines, shotguns, pocket, belt, and repeating pistols, rifle canes, revolving rifles, rifle and shotgun barrels, and gun materials and accessories. In 1867 came the first orders from foreign countries. Denmark, Sweden, Spain, then Egypt, and finally France placed ever larger orders for the Remington breech-loader. In addition the firm filled contracts with the Army and Navy for single shot pistols and rifles. In the 70's Remington arms went to Puerto Rico, Cuba, Chile, Colombia, Honduras, China. And early in those years Remington began large scale manufacture of cartridges and the designing of cartridge machinery.

By 1880 conditions had changed greatly. Foreign countries were establishing their own armories; there were fewer contracts to be had, and those Remington would not secure through the expected bribery. Samuel, who had represented the firm abroad, returned to New York in 1877. To keep the vast plant busy, Remington turned to new lines of manufacture, which, except for the typewriter, proved neither successful nor profitable. Even in the arms field the firm suffered a loss. Remington had given employment and mechanical facilities to inventors for experimentation on repeating long arms with disappointing results. The Keene magazine rifle, developed and manufactured at some expense, failed to measure up to Remington standards and was dropped. A more successful bolt action magazine rifle, the Lee, did not sell in quantity sufficient to cover the loss on the Keene. In December of 1882 Samuel Remington died; his stock in the company was sold to Philo, who became then principal owner as well as manager.

Astute financial direction might have prevented the firm's failure. Philo, pre-eminently a manufacturer, trusted and accepted the advice of men who proved even less competent than himself in financial matters. Neither Philo nor Eliphalet, Jr. were in a position to use private funds to carry the company through growing difficulties; both had made large gifts to educational and philanthropic institutions; Philo had loaned large sums to a friend in spite of his own need. In 1886 the corporation went into receivership. In March 1888 Hartley and Graham of New York, who had organized the Union Metallic Cartridge Company of Bridgeport, Connecticut in 1867, bought a controlling interest. Philo Remington died in April 1889.

From 1888 until 1910 the firm operated under the name "Remington Arms Company." Most of the handgun line was dropped at the outset of this period and efforts concentrated largely on long arms. In 1910 Remington Arms and the Union Metallic Cartridge Company, which had been operating separately though under the same control, were merged. After 1910 only two pistols were manufactured for the general public. In 1920 the corporation, again reorganized, returned to the name "Remington Arms Company," which it still bears. In 1933 E. I. du Pont de Nemours bought controlling interest. By 1935, the two remaining Remington handguns had been discontinued.

Most of the history of the company from 1888 to the present belongs to the Remington long-arms story, a book yet to be published. Today, after the labors of World War II, the oldest firearms manufacturer in the United States is once again supplying the needs of the American hunter and sportsman.

2 ■ ■

THE EARLY HANDGUNS

THE REMINGTON HANDGUN story begins with a flintlock pistol. Although the exact date cannot be established, the first one must have been completed in the very early years of the Remington gun business. Young Eliphalet made pistol as well as rifle barrels from the beginning; he both imported and, later, manufactured locks; he rapidly acquired a group of regular customers for completed guns; and from the very first year, 1816, had Riley Rogers in his employ as a finish gun maker. Since Eliphalet kept few records, the number of flintlock pistols he completed may never be determined. An account still in existence records the sale of one in 1835.[1]

Later in the 1840's and 50's the firm expanded the sale of pistol barrels to gunsmiths and various small concerns in the gun trade. Remington also made complete single shot percussion pistols. Here again, the types and quantities are not known; accounts record only sales.[1]

In 1857 "E. Remington and Sons" began manufacture of a percussion revolver designed and patented by Fordyce Beals, who had first come to Ilion in 1846 in connection with the Jencks carbine contract. It is interesting to note that although Beals was associated with Remington, his first revolver, the famous "Walking Beam" model patented in 1854, was manufactured by Whitney in Connecticut. His second revolver, patented in 1856 and modified by an improvement patented in 1857, was the first of the Remington Beals and the first Remington revolver.

---

[1] These accounts are in the possession of Mr. Loomis, of Ilion, New York.

B E A L S   P O C K E T   R E V O L V E R S

First Model. Beals' patents 15,167, dated June 24, 1856, and 17,359, dated May 26, 1857, cover all the basic features of this gun. In fact, the sketch accompanying the 1857 patent is a true picture of the arm as actually produced. Easily distinguished from later Beals pocket revolvers, the First Model has a smooth, rounded, one-piece composition grip and a round trigger guard, but several have turned up with small two-piece "squarish" wood grips instead of the larger rounded one-piece rubber type. The two-piece grips are held in place by a detachable butt plate. They were apparently offered as a standard alternate since guns with the more conventional grips may still show the tapped holes used to attach the other type.

The cylinder is made to revolve by conventional means, with a "hand" or pawl. The pawl is actuated by an arm which is rigidly attached to the rotating axis of the hammer. This axis, a pin, is keyed to the hammer and moves with it. The mechanism is distinctive in that the arm and part of the pawl are in plain view on the left outside of the frame. When the cylinder is to be removed for loading or cleaning, the cylinder pin is withdrawn forward, leaving the cylinder free to slide out the right side of the frame.

A spring catch, secured by a screw to the upper left of the recoil shield and shaped to fit closely over the bulge of recoil shield and cylinder, serves two functions. It locks the cylinder in position for the discharge when its locking tooth catches in one of the cylinder notches. Since it projects somewhat beyond the recoil shield, the spring also forms a seat into which the cylinder may be inserted rapidly and accurately.

Even on this early model—and on all revolvers throughout the percussion period—Remington used ratchet grooves, instead of the more common teeth, on the rear of the cylinder. Grooves were more reliable, since they were much less subject to wear and deformation under hard usage.

We have, however, seen several of these First Model Beals

with the disc-type pawl of the Second Model. A few were nickel plated.

The German silver cone front sights were made in two sizes; the larger size cone has been found in a semi-blade shape on a few guns.

Markings may appear only on the top of the frame. The majority, however, are stamped on both barrel and frame.

These guns are frequently found in the original cardboard box, complete with brass ball-seater, brass mold and copper flask. The flask may or may not be marked "Remington's, Ilion."

The production figure given is, we suspect, conservative because so many are still in circulation. Since none have been seen with serial numbers over three digits, they undoubtedly were manufactured in "lots" and not numbered from first to last.

One with serial number "32," an early piece carrying only the 1856 patent date, has seven-groove rifling instead of the usual five-groove and is marked on the frame.

Second Model. This revolver, based on the same patents as the First Model and similarly marked with the patent dates, differs from it mainly in external appearance. It has a squarish butt of conventional form and a sheath trigger. A rotating disc replaces the actuating arm first used, but the working principle remains the same. A single-curve main spring supersedes the earlier reverse-curve spring.

Third Model. This is a noticeably larger edition of the Second Model: frame, barrel, and cylinder are all of increased size. It is the only Beals pocket revolver with a lever rammer. Beals patented the lever rammer and base pin combination in 1858; the rammer acts as a base pin retainer and must be lowered before the base pin can be withdrawn. The barrel is usually stamped with all three patent years, '56, '57, '58, but one known specimen carries only the 1858 patent date.

The development of a percussion revolver in the service calibers followed closely upon that of the pocket models (all .31). The Beals Army .44 and Navy .36 acquired their title from the barrel

BEALS' NEW PATENT REVOLVER.

A SUPERIOR ARTICLE,

CARRYING 140 BALLS TO THE POUND,

WEIGHING ONLY ELEVEN OUNCES.

BARRELS AND CYLINDERS OF BEST CAST STEEL.

MANUFACTURED BY

E. REMINGTON & SONS

ILION, N. Y.

The Compactness, Lightness and Simplicity of this Arm, together with the Size of Ball, Range and Penetration, make it one of the most Convenient and Reliable Weapons of Defence that can be found.

The Efficiency of the Arm may be greatly increased by the addition of Duplicate Cylinders, thus affording the advantage of a Brace of Pistols at a trifling additional expense.

DIRECTIONS FOR LOADING.

Half cock the Pistol and draw out the centre pin from the Cylinder, *but not from the Frame.* Take out the Cylinder and charge its Chambers, using no wadding or patch for the balls, which should be driven below the mouths of the Chambers. Percussion Caps should be used of such size as will fit closely to the Cone when pressed down. Replace the Cylinder in the Frame, rolling it in the same direction it revolves in cocking, until the centre pin can be pushed back to its place, when the Pistol is ready for use.

The Balls should be of the softest lead, and none but full and perfect ones should be used. The Powder should also be of the best quality. The Arm should be thoroughly cleaned and oiled after firing.

DIRECTIONS FOR CLEANING.

Take the Cylinder from the Frame, wash it in warm water, dry it thoroughly, oil and replace it in the Frame ; also, oil the Pin upon which the Cylinder revolves.

FANCY WOOD CASES (ARRANGED FOR SINGLE PISTOL OR BRACE,) FURNISHED WHEN DESIRED.

J. W. Orr, Engraver on Wood, 75 Nassau St. N. Y.

Courtesy J. Hintlian

PLATE II.   FROM A PRINTED CIRCULAR—1858.

markings, "Beals Patent Sept. 14, 1858," the famous lever rammer and base pin system patent. The lock arrangement may also have been Beals' or, as with many Remington arms, the combined work of several men. In any event, the pawl was moved to the inside of the frame, producing a more conventional arm. The frame was essentially that of the Third Model pocket, which also used the lever rammer. So the Beals Army and Navy were, in part, the last step in one development while the first of a new line.

BEALS POCKET REVOLVER, THIRD MODEL

An interesting example of the experimenting that went on at the Remington Company is an inventor's model that appeared in the Remington family collection.

In general appearance and styling, the gun follows the Third Model Beals Pocket. It is approximately .28 caliber, with a 24-shot cylinder. The chambers are arranged in two concentric rows in the oversize cylinder. The barrel is pivoted near the muzzle on two slender arms extending forward from the frame; the breech end could be moved up and down to "register" with either row of chambers. Further than this, the operation is not too clear since the specimen was rusty and incomplete. Though unmarked, it is undoubtedly the design of Beals.

BEALS ARMY AND NAVY REVOLVERS

The Beals .44 and .36 caliber revolvers set the general form and mechanical arrangement followed by most Remington hand arms to the end of the percussion period. Even the Frontier (1875) bears a striking resemblance to the Beals Army. The original Beals service revolvers are easily identified: (a) the barrel threads are entirely concealed by the frame; (b) there are no safety notches between nipples; (c) the rammer lever web is very small; (d) the rammer lever must be lowered to withdraw the base pin.

In 1859, Remington, always alert for new firearm inventions, heard of a double-action revolver patented by Joseph Rider, of Newark, Ohio. The company sought out Rider and contracted to manufacture his gun. The connection thus established continued until Rider's retirement; the inventor took up residence in Ilion and, in 1865, became factory superintendent.

A production figure of close to 18,000 has been definitely established for the Beals Navy Revolver. Any number of these revolvers have turned up with serial numbers to 15,000.

There is a noticeable difference between the earliest manufactured and the later "standard" models. Gun number "111" has a single-wing base pin like that of the Beals Third Pocket. Extending from the forward end of this base pin is a tiny, integral rod about one-sixteenth inch in diameter and one and one-half inches in length. The little rod fits into a machined slot in the upper rear surface of the rammer lever and is concealed when the lever is latched. The exact purpose of the pin remains obscure; it does not appear in later guns.

The early models also have a slightly longer rammer latch.

RIDER POCKET REVOLVER

The construction and operation of this model are detailed in Rider's patents of August 17, 1858, No. 21,215, and May 3, 1859, No. 23,861. Even without the unusual "mushroom" cylinder, the gun's distinctive outline identifies it at a glance. One of the earliest double-action revolvers, it proved exceedingly popular and sold, in conversion form, as late as 1888. The Government bought considerable numbers of them during the Civil War and issued them as pocket weapons.

Two conversions with original barrels only two inches long have turned up in private collections.

RIDER DERRINGER

Rider's patent for this pistol is dated September 13, 1859 (patent No. 25,470). Barrel, frame, and right grip are integral, machined from one piece of brass. A removable plate fills out the left side of the grip and part of the frame. The brass barrel, smooth bore, and miniature caliber (.170) are decidedly unusual in a Remington handgun; the mechanism is unique. The breech end of the barrel is counterbored or chambered to receive, in order, a ball, a cap tube with percussion cap thereon, and a hollow breech-pin. The breech-pin arm, an integral part extending from the rear at right angles, fits down into an oversize slot in the right side of the frame. No gunpowder is used in the charge. In firing, the hammer descends on the breech-pin, sliding it forward and discharging the cap; the force of the cap explosion propels the ball.

1861 ARMY AND NAVY REVOLVERS

The 1861 service revolvers are, essentially, an attempt to improve the Beals. Oddly enough, the principal change is a definite departure from the Beals 1858 patent. These arms incorporate Wm. H. Elliot's patent No. 33,932 dated December 17, 1861 for a system whereby the base pin can be withdrawn without unlatching the lever rammer. When in its rearward position, the base pin is held in place by a friction spring. When drawn forward, two grooves in the head ride on the sides of the lever rammer while the round pin itself rides in a channel in the upper surface of the lever. For about two-thirds of the distance between frame and catch the lever rammer is cut away just enough to allow passage for the metal attaching the thumb wings to the main body of the base pin. As a result, a distinct air space can be observed between barrel and lever. The 1861 is the only model in which there is no frame cut-out for the base pin wings. It is the first model in which the barrel threads are visible, the last manufactured exhibiting this feature.

The Elliot lever rammer proved impractical, and in some of the 1861's a screw was fixed in the lever channel so that the base pin could not be withdrawn without lowering the rammer. New Model cylinders with safety notches were installed in a few.

In 1863 Remington brought out the New Model revolvers, the last of the cap-and-ball handguns. The culmination of a relatively brief period of experiment and improvement, the New Model line represents, in our opinion, the highest development of the percussion revolver.

The estimate of total production of the Model 1861 Army Revolver is now "over 10,000."

On the basis of an extensive (and continuing) study of serial numbers and models, total production of the 1861 Navy reached close to 22,000.

Serial number "21,532" is a very late transition revolver: markings, rammer lever and hammer are 1861 style, but cylinder and grips are New Model. The assembly is obviously original.

NEW MODEL ARMY AND NAVY

The New Model .44 and .36, correcting the faults of both the Beals and the 1861's, might also be called the third models. The lever rammer and base pin arrangement is a refinement of the original Beals patent: the rammer must be lowered to withdraw the base pin; the base pin can be drawn forward only far enough to free the cylinder. The construction that prevents the base pin from being entirely withdrawn, although present in rudimentary form on earlier guns, is Samuel Remington's patent No. 37,921 of March 17, 1863. Some of the New Models are stamped with the 1863 patent date and others are not, but the patent applies to all of them.

For the first time "safety" notches are used on the rear radius of the cylinder. These notches, cut midway between nipple seats, provide a safe resting place for the hammer nose when the arm is uncocked and not in use. From a design standpoint, the addition of safety notches is the most noteworthy of the improvements that appear on the New Models. The .44 has an iron front sight which screws into the barrel; most of the .36's retain the brass or German

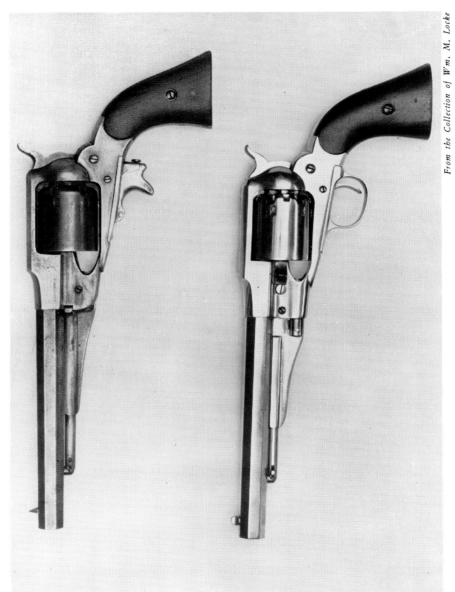

PLATE III.

silver cone front sight with dovetail base, standard on previous Remington handguns.

Our original theory that the New Model Armies and Navies did not start with serial number "1" in either case, but took up where the 1861 Armies and Navies left off, continuing with no break, has been confirmed. An intensive search revealed lower and lower New Model numbers, down to certain breakpoints; the recorded 1861 numbers crept higher and higher, but never quite to the New Model numbers. The transition was gradual, not abrupt. New Model .44's numbers "19,793" and "19,981" both have the early German silver cone front sights of the 1861 and lack the actual stamp "New Model."

Recorded Serial Number Spread

1861 Army	6,494 to	10,446
New Model Army	19,793 to	147,283
1861 Navy	2,044 to	21,532
New Model Navy	24,246 to	44,943

Remington toyed with the idea of a shoulder-stock for the New Model .44 but apparently never got the item beyond the development stage. The stocked New Model that we owned was serial number "58,018," dating it generally as mid-Civil War. The lower third of each grip had been sawed off; over the empty space thus left, a bronze split-clamp type of attachment was fitted. The clamp had rifle style tangs which held a conventional light stock. Workmanship was typically "model shop," but still beyond the means of a basement mechanic. Another .44, rigged to take this type of stock, but with the stock missing, had grip-shaped metal pieces fitting over the blank space.

Since two guns, both adapted to the same unusual method of stocking, and both plainly factory made, have turned up in widely separated places, there is no reason to question that these are examples of one of Remington's known experiments in shoulder stocking handguns.

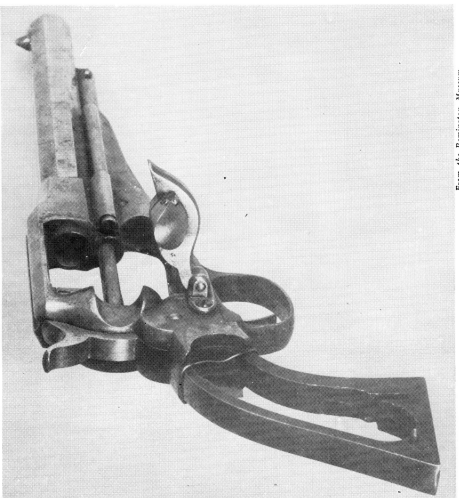

A number of men, the most notable being William H. Elliot and Samuel Remington, devoted some time and effort to refining the Remington Army revolvers. Elliot seems to have done considerable work particularly in the development of a faster and more efficient method of inserting and removing the base pin and cylinder. His patent 47,707, of May 16, 1865, was one result. An unmarked .44 (Figure b, Plate III) similar in operation to the patent, is close enough to suggest the same origin.

Another .44, stamped only "J. Birkenhead," embodies a very odd trigger "sheath," or housing. Forward pressure on the little button releases the housing, which drops down and exposes the trigger (Figure a, Plate III).

Trigger guards were nickel plated on a few otherwise standard high-number New Model .44's; the significance, if any, escapes us.

The ejector rod preceded the loading gate in development of the final conversion style of large service model percussion revolvers. Plate IV illustrates an experimental model of loading gate.

NEW MODEL BELT

Single Action. This is a somewhat smaller version of the Navy 36. Other than size, the only difference is that the screws enter from the right side of the frame. A blade front sight is standard.

Double Action. In common with the Rider Pocket, the double-action lock of this gun is based on Rider's patents 21,215 of August 17, 1858 and 23,861 of May 3, 1859. The position of the trigger and the brass cone front sight are the only striking features to distinguish it at a casual glance from the single action.

The double-action belt with full fluted cylinder made on special customer order has sometimes been set apart from the one with standard round cylinder and both incorrectly titled "Navy" arms. The type of cylinder found on a Remington revolver is not a sound basis on which to establish a particular "model"; on order, Remington would furnish a full fluted cylinder for any given arm.

There is no record of any Navy purchase of the double-action belt, either with or without a fluted cylinder.

N E W   M O D E L   P O L I C E

This is a second and further reduction in size of the pattern established by the service revolvers. The caliber remains at .36 as in the Navy and Belt; the number of chambers is dropped from six to five. Hammer and trigger screws enter from the right side of the frame. The front sight is a brass blade.

N E W   M O D E L   P O C K E T

The smallest of the New Models, this is the only one with a sheath trigger. A resemblance to the Third Model Beals Pocket is noticeable though the gun is typically New Model in construction and appearance.

R E V O L V I N G   R I F L E

Although a long arm, the revolving rifle belongs in this chapter because it is essentially a revolver, made with rifle barrel and shoulder stock. Frame, cylinder, and lever rammer-base pin are identical in construction with the New Model service revolvers. Made in both .36 and .44, the revolving rifle appears in conversion form in catalogs as late as 1879.

3 ■ ■

CATALOG OF PERCUSSION MODELS

THE MODEL designations are, in most cases, those originally given the arms by the Remington Company. Where Remington used several titles for the same arm, the authors have tried to choose the most accurate and descriptive. Where the Remington title was vague or applied to several arms, the authors have adopted the designation generally accepted by collectors.

Years of manufacture were determined on the basis of patent dates stamped on arms, known sales and contracts, and Remington catalogs and advertisements. Estimates of the number manufactured of the various models are based on known contracts and sales, known statements of the company in the past, probable rates of production, and known serial numbers. These estimates were arrived at by the authors in collaboration with Mr. Loomis. Since none of the material used in making these estimates is the property of the Remington Arms Company, although much of it was made available through their co-operation, they understandably do not wish to be held officially responsible for the accuracy of the figures.

PLATE V.
BEALS POCKET REVOLVER, FIRST MODEL
(Single Action)

Caliber: .31
Barrel: 3" octagon
Cylinder: 1¼" long
Number of shots: 5
Rifling: 5 or 7 grooves
Trigger guard: round, brass
Sights: front, German silver cone; rear, groove
Grips: composition, rounded, smooth
Finish: blued barrel, frame, cylinder; case hardened hammer; silver plated trigger guard

Weight: 11 ounces
Distinctive feature: Outside pawl and arm
Markings—
Top of barrel: F. BEAL'S PATENT, JUNE 24, '56 & MAY 26, '57
Top of frame: REMINGTONS, ILION, N. Y.
Serial number: inside of trigger guard; on butt; on grip frame
Dates of manufacture: 1857-1858
Number manufactured: Estimated at 2500

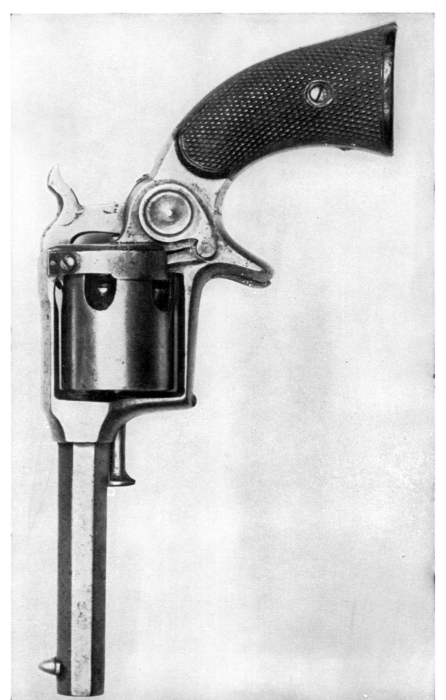

From the collection of Mr. Girard Chambers, of Hampton, Virginia

PLATE VI.
BEALS POCKET REVOLVER, SECOND MODEL
(Single Action)

Caliber: .31
Barrel: 3" octagon
Cylinder: 1⅛" long
Number of shots: 5
Rifling: 5 grooves
Trigger: sheath
Sights: front, German silver cone; *rear,* groove
Grips: hard rubber, checkered

Finish: blued
Weight: 12 ounces
Distinctive feature: outside pawl and disc
Markings—
   Top of barrel: BEALS PATENT 1856 & 57. MANUFAC-
      TURED BY REMINGTON, ILION, N. Y.
Serial number: underside of barrel; side of grip frame
Dates of manufacture: 1858-1850
Number manufactured: Estimated at 1,000

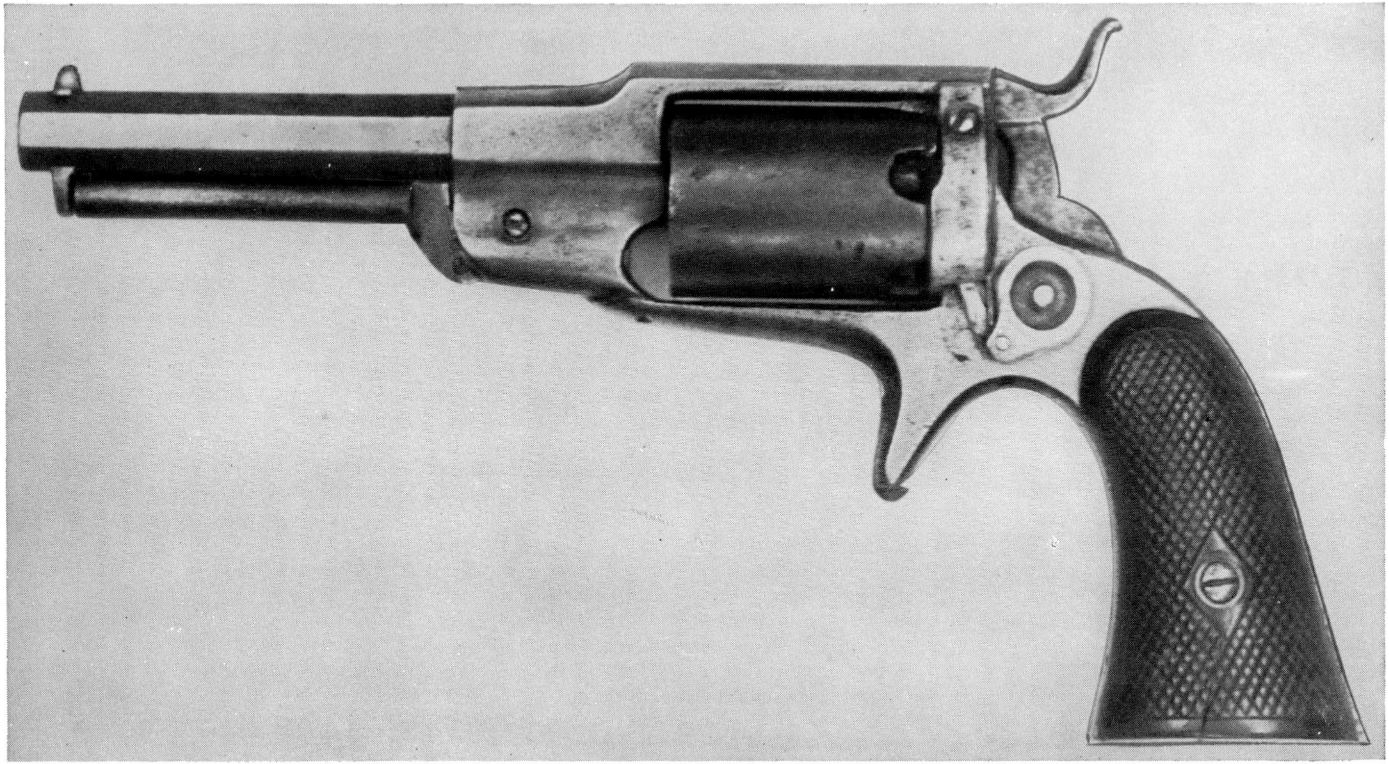

From the Chambers collection

PLATE VII.
BEALS POCKET REVOLVER, THIRD MODEL
(Single Action)

Caliber: .31
Barrel: 4" octagon
Cylinder: 1⅝" long
Number of shots: 5
Rifling: 5 grooves
Trigger: sheath
Sights: front, German silver cone; *rear* groove
Grips: hard rubber, checkered

Finish: blued
Weight: 14 ounces
Distinctive features: outside pawl and disc; lever rammer
Markings—
    Top of barrel: BEALS PAT. 1856, 57, 58: MANUFAC-
        TURED BY REMINGTON, ILION, N .Y.
Serial number: side of grip frame
Dates of manufacture: 1859-1860
Number manufactured: estimated at 1,500

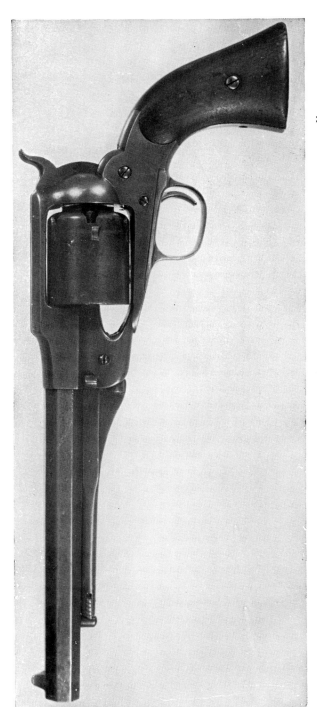

PLATE VIII.
BEALS ARMY REVOLVER
(Single Action)

Caliber: .44
Barrel: 8" octagon
Cylinder: 2" long
Number of shots: 6
Rifling: 5 grooves
Trigger guard: brass oval
Sights: front, German silver cone; rear, groove
Grips: walnut, oil finished

Finish: blued, except case-hardened hammer
Weight: 2 pounds, 14 ounces
Distinctive feature: small lever rammer web
Markings—
Top of barrel: BEALS PATENT SEPT. 14, 1858 MANU-
FACTURED BY REMINGTON'S ILION, NEW YORK
Serial number: underside of barrel; side of grip frame
Dates of manufacture: 1860-1862
Number manufactured: estimated at 3,000

Moore

PLATE IX.
BEALS NAVY REVOLVER
(Single Action)

Caliber: .36
Barrel: 7½" octagon
Cylinder: 2" long
Number of shots: 6
Rifling: 5 grooves
Trigger guard: brass, oval
Sights: front, German silver cone; rear, groove
Grips: walnut, oil finished

Finish: blued, except case-hardened hammer
Weight: 2 pounds, 10 ounces
Distinctive feature: small lever rammer web
Markings—
    Top of barrel: BEALS PATENT SEPT. 14, 1858 MANU-
        FACTURED BY REMINGTON ILION, NEW YORK
Serial number: underside of barrel; side of grip frame
Dates of manufacture: 1860-1862
Number manufactured: over 8,000

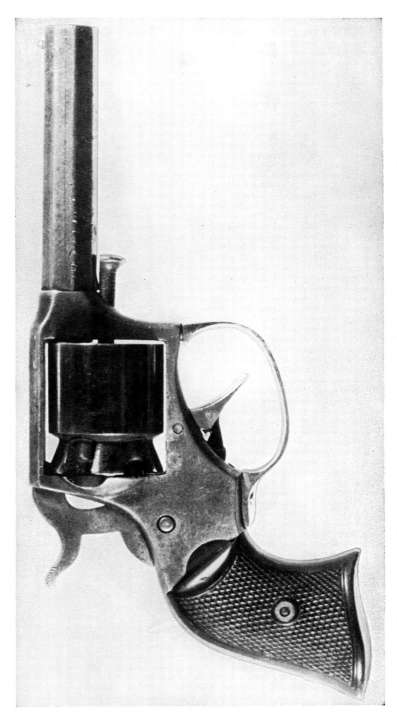

Moore

PLATE X.
RIDER POCKET REVOLVER
(Double Action)

Caliber: .31
Barrel: 3" octagon
Cylinder: 1¼" long
Number of shots: 5
Rifling: 5 grooves
Trigger guard: large oval, brass
Sights: front, brass pin; *rear,* groove
Grips: hard rubber, checkered; pearl; ivory
Finish: blued; nickel plated frame; full nickel plated
Weight: 10 ounces

Distinctive features: "mushroom" cylinder; large trigger guard; straight trigger
Markings—
 Top of barrel: MANUFACTURED BY REMINGTON'S, ILION, N. Y., RIDERS PT. AUG. 17, 1858 MAY 3, 1859
Serial number: underside of barrel; on frame inside trigger guard
Dates of manufacture: 1860-1888
Number manufactured: estimated at over 100,000

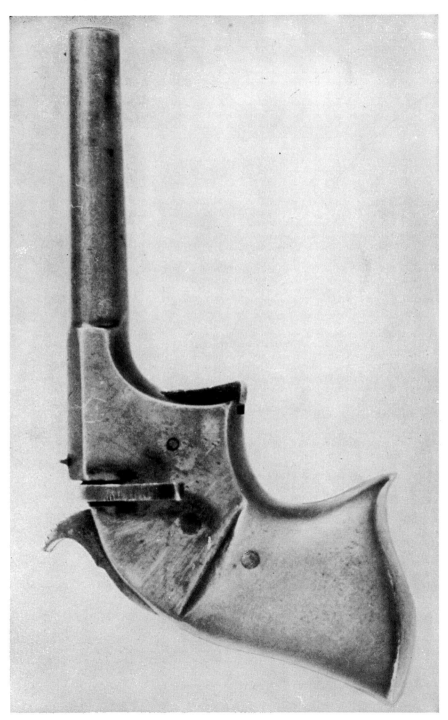

Moore

PLATE XI.
RIDER SINGLE SHOT DERRINGER
(Single Action)

Caliber: .170
Barrel: 3" round, brass, integral with frame
Rifling: none
Trigger: sheath. *Parts:* iron hammer; steel breech-pin
Sights: front, brass pin; *rear,* V-notch
Grips: brass, smooth, integral with frame

Finish: natural brass
Weight: 5⅜ ounces
Markings—
  Top of barrel: RIDERS PT. SEPT. 13, 1859
Dates of manufacture: 1860-1863
Number manufactured: estimated at less than 1,000

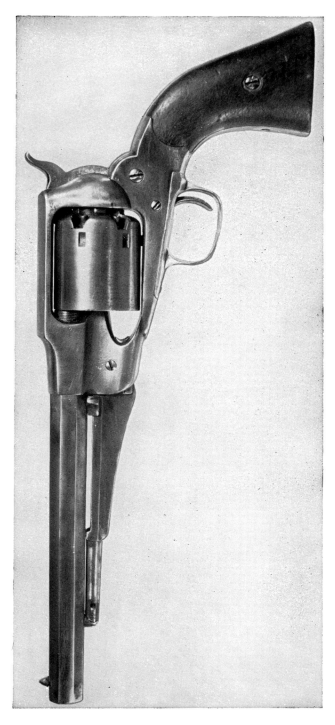

From the authors' collection

Moore

PLATE XII.
MODEL 1861 ARMY REVOLVER
(Single Action)

Caliber: .44
Barrel: 8" octagon
Cylinder: 2" long
Number of shots: 6
Rifling: 5 grooves
Trigger guard: brass, oval
Sights: front, German silver cone: rear, groove
Grips: walnut, oil finished
Finish: blued, except for case-hardened hammer

Weight: 2 pounds, 12 ounces
Distinctive features: channel in rammer lever; noticeable space between lever and barrel
Markings—
Top of barrel: PATENTED DEC. 17, 1861, MANUFACTURED BY REMINGTON'S, ILION, N. Y.
Serial number: underside of barrel; side of grip frame
Dates of manufacture: 1862
Number manufactured: over 5,000

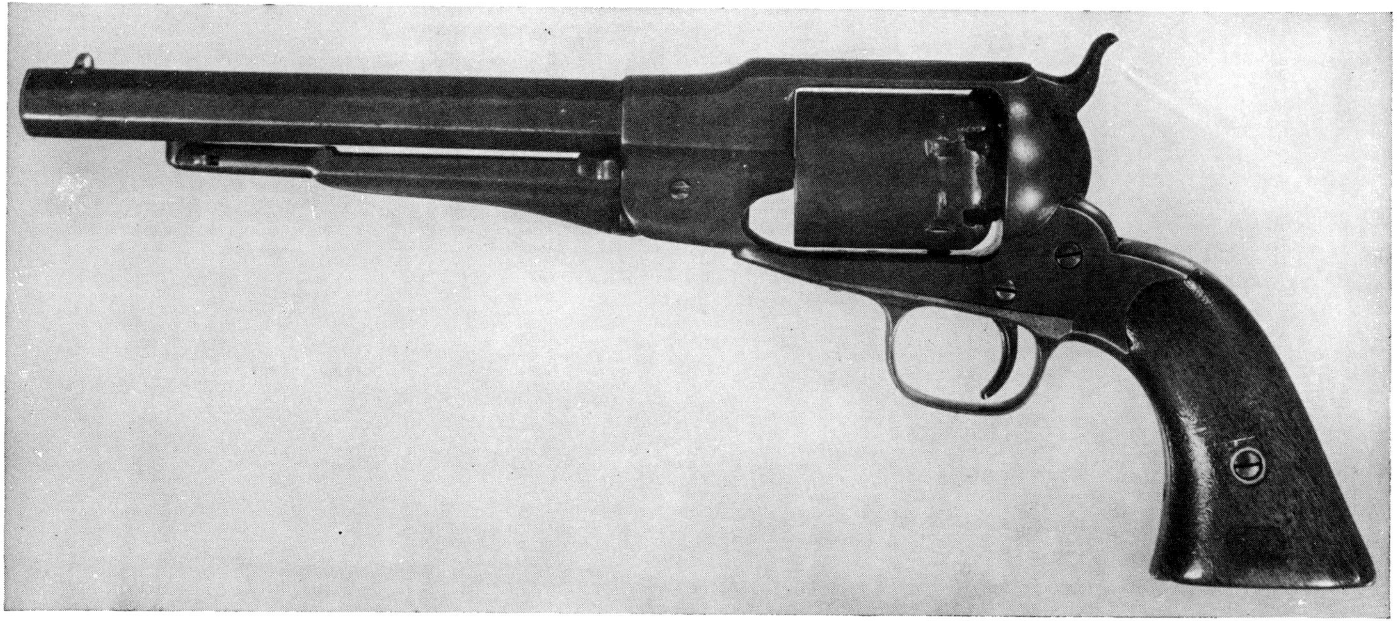

From the collection of Mr. Roger Peterson, of Portland, Maine *Moore*

PLATE XIII.
MODEL 1861 NAVY REVOLVER
(Single Action)

Caliber: .36
Barrel: 7⅜" octagon
Cylinder: 2" long
Number of shots: 6
Rifling: 5 grooves
Trigger guard: brass, oval
Sights: front, German silver cone; rear, groove
Grips: walnut, oil finished
Finish: blued, except for case-hardened hammer

Weight: 2 pounds, 8 ounces
Distinctive features: channel in rammer lever; noticeable space between lever and barrel
Markings—
Top of barrel: PATENTED DEC. 17, 1861. MANUFAC-TURED BY REMINGTON'S, ILION, N. Y.
Serial number: underside of barrel; side of grip frame
Dates of manufacture: 1862
Number manufactured: over 5,000

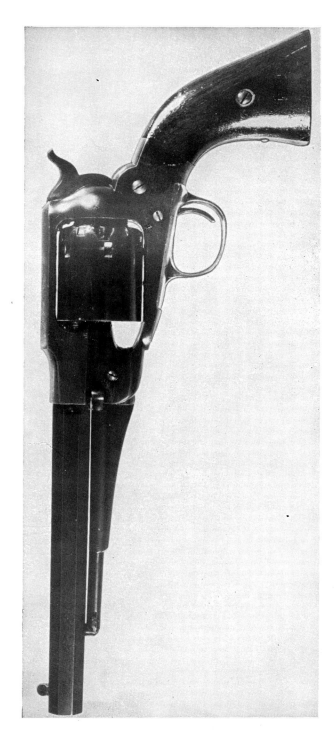

PLATE XIV.

NEW MODEL ARMY REVOLVER
(Single Action)

Caliber: .44
Barrel: 8" octagon
Cylinder: 2" long
Number of shots: 6
Rifling: 5 grooves
Trigger guard: brass, oval
Sights: front, iron blade; *rear,* groove
Grips: walnut, oil finished
Finish: blued, except for case-hardened hammer
Weight: 2 pounds, 14 ounces

Markings—
Top of barrel: PATENTED SEPT. 14, 1858. E. REMING-TON & SONS, ILION, NEW YORK, U.S.A. NEW MODEL

Left grip: inspector's initials in script in rectangle (B.H and O.W.A. have been noted)

Serial number: underside of barrel; side of grip frame
Dates of manufacture: 1863-1875
Number Manufactured: Over 140,000

Note: Standard New Model .44's sold to the general public came with blued finish and varnished grips; plated or engraved pieces with pearl or ivory grips could be purchased at extra cost.

From the collection of Mr. Roger Peterson, of Portland, Maine *Moore*

PLATE XV.
NEW MODEL NAVY REVOLVER
(Single Action)

Caliber: .36
Barrel: 7⅜" octagon
Cylinder: 2" long
Number of shots: 6
Rifling: 5 grooves
Trigger guard: brass, oval
Sights: *front,* German silver cone or iron blade; *rear,* groove
Grips: walnut, oil finished
Finish: blued, except for case-hardened hammer
Weight: 2 pounds, 10 ounces

Markings—
Top of barrel: PATENTED SEPT. 14, 1858. E. REMINGTON & SONS, ILION, NEW YORK, U.S.A. NEW MODEL
Left grip: inspector's initials in script in rectangle
Serial number: underside of barrel; side of grip frame
Dates of manufacture: 1863-1888
Number manufactured: over 32,000

Note: Standard New Model .36's sold to the general public came with blued finish and varnished grips; plated or engraved pieces with pearl or ivory grips could be purchased at extra cost.

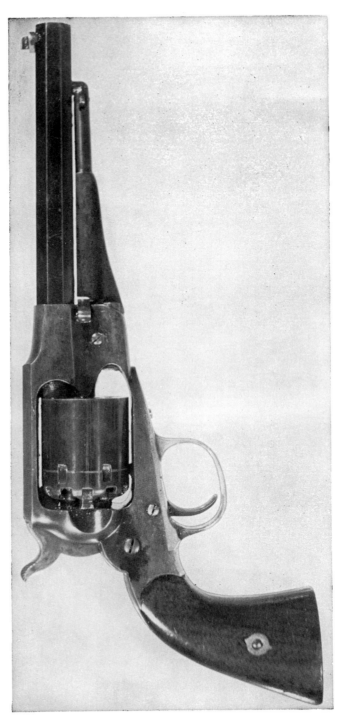

Moore

From the authors' collection

PLATE XVI.
NEW MODEL BELT REVOLVER
(Single Action)

Caliber: .36
Barrel: 6½" octagon
Cylinder: 1⅞" long
Number of shots: 6
Rifling: 5 grooves
Trigger guard: brass, oval
Sights: front, German silver blade; rear, groove
Grips: walnut, varnished; pearl; ivory
Finish: blued; nickel plated frame; full nickel plated; specially
plated or engraved on order

Weight: 2 pounds, 2 ounces
Markings—
Top of barrel: PATENTED SEPT. 14, 1858. E. REMING-
TON & SONS, ILION, NEW YORK U.S.A. NEW
MODEL
Serial number: underside of barrel; side of grip frame
Dates of manufacture: 1863-1888
Number manufactured: no records, but serial numbers over
5,000 have been observed

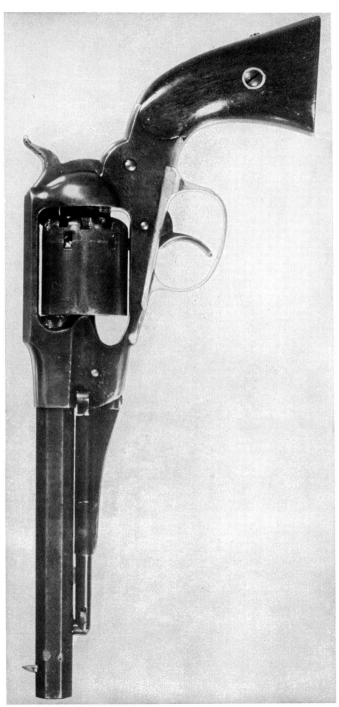

PLATE XVII.
NEW MODEL BELT REVOLVER
(Double Action)

Caliber: .36
Barrel: 6½" octagon
Cylinder: 1⅞" long
Number of shots: 6
Rifling: 5 grooves
Trigger guard: brass, oval
Sights: front, German silver cone; rear, groove
Grips: walnut, varnished; pearl; ivory
Finish: blued; nickel plated frame; full nickel plated; specially plated or engraved on order

Weight: 2 pounds, 4 ounces
Markings—
Top of barrel: MANUFACTURED BY REMINGTON'S, ILION, N. Y. RIDER'S PT. AUG. 17, 1858, MAY 3, 1859 (or standard New Model marking)
Serial number: underside of barrel; side of grip frame
Dates of manufacture: 1863-1888
Number manufactured: no records, but serial numbers over 5,000 have been observed
Note: Full fluted cylinder on special order.

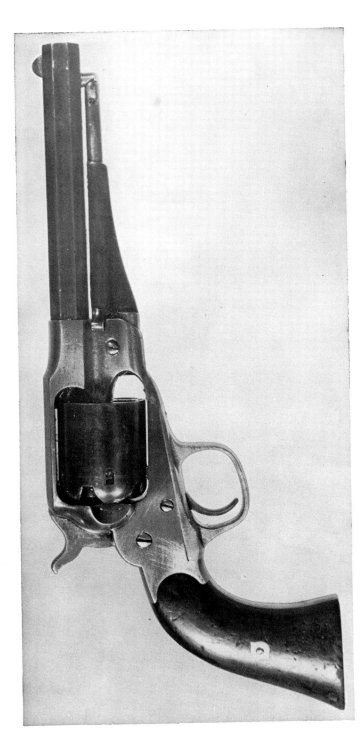

PLATE XVIII.
NEW MODEL POLICE REVOLVER
(Single Action)

Caliber: .36
Barrel: 3½", 4½", 5½", 6½" octagon
Cylinder: 1⅝" long
Number of shots: 5
Rifling: 5 grooves
Trigger guard: brass, oval
Sights: front, German silver blade; rear, groove
Grips: walnut varnished; pearl; ivory
Finish: blued; nickel plated frame; full nickel plated; specially plated or engraved on order

Weight: 21, 22, 23, 24 ounces
Markings—
Top of barrel: PATENTED SEPT. 14, 1858 MARCH 17, 1863 E. REMINGTON & SONS, ILION, NEW YORK
U.S.A. NEW MODEL
Serial number: underside of barrel; side of grip frame
Dates of manufacture: 1863-1888
Number manufactured: no records, but serial numbers over 8,000 have been observed

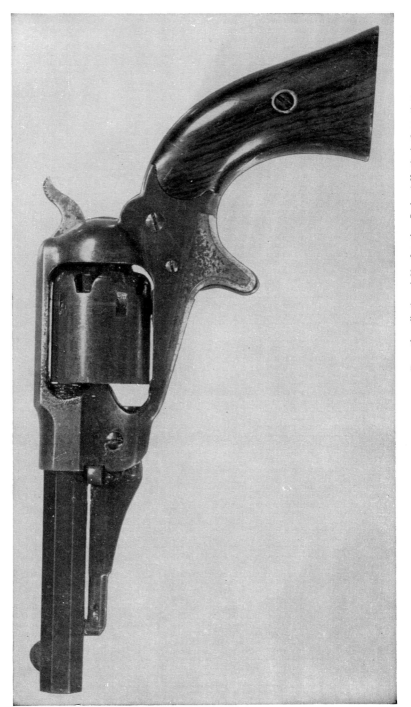

PLATE XIX.
NEW MODEL POCKET REVOLVER
(Single Action)

Caliber: .31
Barrel: 3½", 4½" octagon
Cylinder: 1 7/16" long
Number of shots: 5
Rifling: 5 grooves
Trigger: sheath
Sights: front, German silver blade; rear, groove
Grips: walnut, varnished; pearl; ivory
Finish: blued; nickel plated frame; full nickel plated; specially
plated or engraved on order

Weight: 14, 16 ounces
Markings—
Top of barrel: PATENTED SEPT. 14, 1858 MARCH 17,
1863 E. REMINGTON & SONS, ILION, NEW YORK
U.S.A. NEW MODEL
Serial number: underside of barrel; side of grip frame
Dates of manufacture: 1863-1888
Number manufactured: no records, but serial numbers over
17,000 have been observed

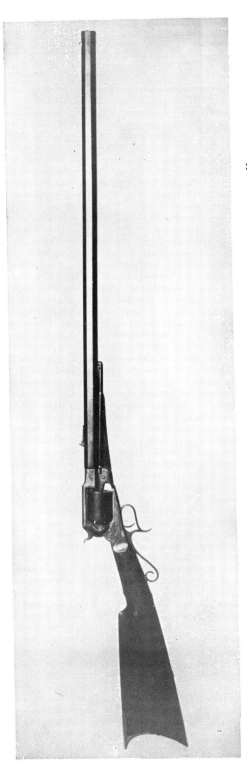

From the Remington Museum

Moore

PLATE XX.
REVOLVING RIFLE
(Single Action)

Caliber: .36; .44
Barrel: 24", 26", 28" half-octagon or full octagon
Cylinder: 2" long
Number of shots: 6
Rifling: 5 grooves
Trigger guard: brass, scroll
Sights: front, German silver bead; *rear,* buckhorn
Stock: walnut varnished

Finish: blued
Weight: 6 pounds; 6 pounds, 5 ounces; 6 pounds, 10 ounces
Markings—
    Top of barrel: PATENTED SEPT. 14, 1858 E. REMING-
        TON & SONS, ILION, NEW YORK, U.S.A. NEW
        MODEL
Serial number: underside of barrel
Dates of manufacture: 1866-1879
Number manufactured: estimated at less than 3,000

From the authors' collection

Moore

PLATE XXI.   THE NEW MODEL ARMY .44.

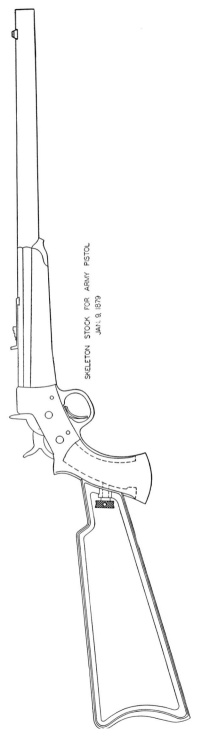

SKELETON STOCK FOR ARMY PISTOL
JAN. 9, 1879

From a factory sketch

PLATE XXII.
MODEL 1879 ARMY
(Single Action)

Caliber: .44 center fire
Number of shots: 1
Barrel: 16" half-octagon
Rifling: 5 grooves
Trigger guard: iron, oval
Sights: front, iron blade; *rear,* buckhorn

Grips: walnut, oil finished
Finish: blued
Weight: not known
Markings—
    Not known
Date of manufacture: 1879
Number manufactured: no record

4 ▪ ▪

CONVERSIONS

THE HYBRID FIREARMS called conversions, produced during the twenty year period following the Civil War, are of special interest to many collectors. A conversion, as the term is used in this book, is any gun designed originally for powder and ball and reworked or refitted to take cartridges.

Actually, by 1865 probably all manufacturers possessed the technical information necessary to produce cartridge revolvers as such. Existing patents, large stocks of percussion guns and parts, and customer conservatism and economy operated toward both continued use of percussion models and extensive conversion. Although the Remington Company advertised factory converted handguns as early as 1866, their catalogs as late as 1888 offered revolvers with the option of a percussion cylinder. Many Remington customers who did adopt the cartridge type arm in its early years returned their percussion guns to the factory for conversion. This procedure was only natural, since it was cheaper than purchasing a new revolver. With the factory altering both individual customers' guns and its own stock, it is easy to understand why so many conversions appear on the antique firearms market today.

Remington developed two methods of converting the Army and Navy service revolvers. The New Model Army .44 (Plate XXI) illustrates the first of these. The percussion cylinder was discarded. A new cylinder, with chambers recessed for cartridge rims and notches providing entrance for the hammer nose, was installed. The new five shot cylinder took a .46 rim fire shell. A thin spacer

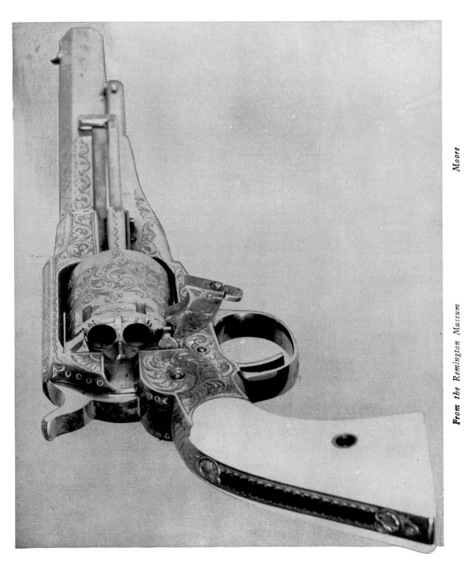

Moore

PLATE XXIII.   THE NAVY .36.

plate was fastened by screws to the forward surface of the recoil shield. Minor work was done on the nose of the hammer and on the hand. An enlarged cut-out in the right half of the recoil shield provided a channel for loading and ejecting the shells. The old lever rammer was left in place and no ejector added.

Remington catalogs described the service models converted by the succeeding method as the "Improved Army" and "Improved Navy" revolvers. The Army .44 was again furnished with a new five shot, .46 rim fire cylinder. In this conversion, the entire recoil shield was removed from both sides of the frame and a deep loading groove cut in the right side. A quarter-inch thick spacer plate, of cylinder size, was fitted between the breech end of the cylinder and the frame. The right half of this plate contained within itself a latched loading gate. A side rod ejector was installed on the right. The Navy .36, similarly altered to .38 rim fire or .38 center fire, was equipped with a new six shot cylinder. (See Plate XXIII.)

The smaller percussion pocket and belt revolvers were converted in the manner illustrated in Plate XXIV. A new cylinder was recessed and notched for rim fire cartridges. A removable base plate, added to the rear of the cylinder, acted as both spacer and cartridge retainer. Cylinder rotating grooves were milled in this plate as well as safety notches between chambers. A positive lock between cylinder and plate was obtained with the use of a central collar and an index pin. No loading channel or rod ejector was provided; the cylinder must be removed for ejection and reloading.

The revolvers altered by this method were suitable for use with either a cartridge or a percussion cylinder. Lever rammers were retained for use with the latter. The extreme nose of the hammer would fire a rim fire cartridge; the portion just beneath the nose, a percussion cap. These arms were advertised and sold with either or both types of cylinder until 1888. Obviously, a lingering public demand for percussion handguns must have been responsible for the long retention of this system. The reasons for that demand are understandable. The early cartridges were naturally far from perfect, apt to misfire, rupture cases, or stick in

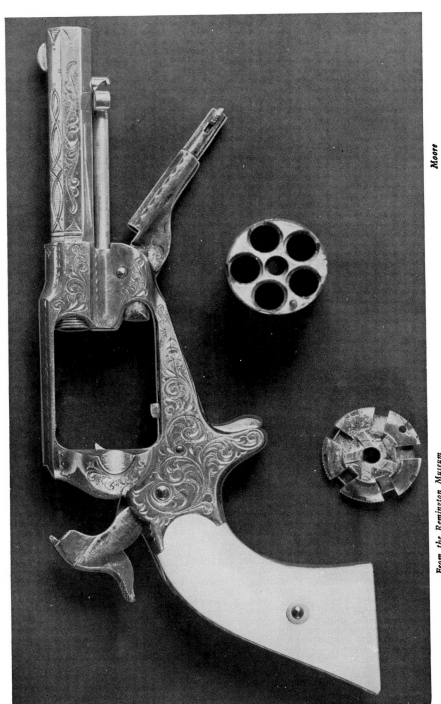

From the Remington Museum

PLATE XXIV.   A CONVERTED PERCUSSION POCKET REVOLVER.

the chamber. And, of course, powder, caps, and lead provided cheaper shooting than fixed ammunition.

The conversions described were the three principal types of alteration done at the Remington factory. Others may well have been produced either as factory experiments or on special order. Their importance, except to collectors of oddities or experimental models, is questioned. Nor are alterations by private gunsmiths or individuals considered here.

NEW MODEL POCKET REVOLVER

A presentation conversion of this model in the Remington family collection carried the serial number "18,270." Another specimen, otherwise standard, had a bronze frame.

5 ■ ■

THE CARTRIDGE MODELS

THE FIRST OF THE REMINGTON cartridge models, the unusual Zig-Zag Derringer, was a design and patent of Wm. H. Elliot. Whether Elliot was one of the inventors who came to Ilion on their own or one of those brought by Remington is not too clear. He was hired full time in 1860 and remained with Remington until 1886.

ZIG-ZAG DERRINGER

William H. Elliot's patents 21,188 of August 17, 1858 and 28,461 of May 29, 1860, on which the Zig-Zag is based, illustrate the rapid arms development of the period. The first describes, actually, a small percussion pepperbox with pin ratchet mechanism; the second, a cartridge gun operating on the principle of the inclined plane.

The piece is double action: when the trigger is pushed forward and pulled back, one cycle of revolving, cocking, and firing, is completed. Examination of the outer surface of the barrel cluster (cylinder) reveals a series of straight fore and aft grooves connected by slanting grooves. On the forward motion of the trigger, a stud rides forward in one of the straight grooves; in the rearward travel of the trigger, the stud enters a slanting groove, causing rotary motion of the barrels. While the barrels revolve, the hammer is being cammed to full-cock; near the end of the backward stroke it is released, firing a cartridge. A circular port in the breech plate provides for loading and ejecting the shells.

Produced for a limited time only, the Zig-Zag was superseded by other models more rugged and more easily manufactured.

REMINGTON-ELLIOT DERRINGER

Wm. Elliot's patents, No. 28,460 of May 29, 1860 and No. 33,832 of October 1, 1861, form the design basis of this model. Two types were made: a five shot .22 with round barrel cluster; a slightly larger and heavier four shot .32 with square barrel cluster.

The arm is double action: a push and pull on the ring trigger completes one cycle of operation. This mechanism is based on stationary barrels and a revolving firing pin. A downward moving pawl, operating on a four or five arm ratchet, rotates the firing pin to successive positions. Another pawl, linked to the trigger and operating on the backward stroke, brings the hammer to full cock. At rest, so to speak, the hammer does not touch the firing pin, and it, in turn, is held away from the cartridge heads by a light coil spring. The barrel assembly drops for loading when released by a sliding catch just forward of the trigger.

The four shot .32 was carried as a sidearm by officers in the Civil War. At least one known specimen is London proof marked, and there are probably others. In 1864 and 1865 Elliot took out three different patents, all for projected improvements on this basic model. Examination of the papers indicates that probable fabrication costs, if not the complication itself, prevented their adoption.

VEST POCKET PISTOL .22

Strangely enough, Elliot's patent No. 33,382 dated October 1, 1861 also includes the main feature of the Vest Pocket .22. Paragraphs No. 3 and No. 5 of that patent cover a hammer hung underneath and forward of the rear end of a chamber. Further, the hammer is so arranged that it does double duty as a striker and a breech block. Such an action is quite suitable for the low pressure involved. Very few developments were necessary to turn the fundamental idea into a practical and inexpensive pocket .22. The absurdly simple mechanism, small size, and low cost caught public fancy and the arm was popular for many years. The caliber and

FULL SIZE.

ELLIOT'S POCKET REPEATER,

The most Compact, Safe and Powerful Revolver ever made. It is charged with common Metallic Cartridges, No. 2, or 32. Barrels Rifled with Gain Twist and Sighted. Carries four heavy Charges.

(62)

THE Barrels of this Pistol are as long as those of ordinary pocket revolvers, yet owing to its peculiar arrangement, while it occupies less than one third the space of any other of equal efficiency, it avoids the loss of power from the open joint in all pistols in which revolving cylinders are used, and is therefore twenty per cent more powerful than such pistols with the same cartridge and same length of barrel.

It has every advantage of a pistol that is cocked by the thumb, as the hammer can be raised to full cock by the trigger, and held so without effort, when correct sight may be taken and the pistol fired at leisure; or it may be cocked and fired instantaneously.

Its arrangement is entirely novel and distinct from the Revolvers heretofore made, which though great improvements in their day, and much improved upon from time to time, are called the complicated machinery, having the same cylinder, with its disadvantages and cumbersome and complicated machinery, all worse than unnecessary, on account of their weight, size, liability to get out of order, and great loss of power in the joint between cylinder and barrel; the ascertained amount of less is one fifth in using the smallest possible cartridge, and then with the same length of barrel is more than twice as large as the Elliot Pistol using the large cartridge.

A very important feature in the Elliot Repeater is its entire safety, there is no chance of an accidental discharge, the parts are so few and simple that they are easily placed inside the handle, the hammer is thus protected and cannot be reached except fixed in the regular way. When fired the hammer half cocks again, withdrawing the "firing point" behind the breech plate, out of reach of the cartridge.

It occupies no space but for barrel and handle, can be carried in a watch pocket of ordinary size where its weight is not felt. Its penetration is three inches of pine, with the long cartridge.

It is fired more rapidly than other Pistols, by simply moving the ring trigger forward and back with the first finger, holding the second firmly around the handle.

Is loaded quicker than others. The barrels are tipped up, the cartridge inserted and barrels bolted down.

It has longer barrels than the Derringer, and like it gets the whole power of the cartridge, there is no escape of gas until the ball is forced out of the muzzle.

☞ Persons purchasing these pistols will be allowed twenty four hours to try them. If not satisfied they may return them, and the money will be refunded.

THE TRADE SUPPLIED

AN EARLY REMINGTON CIRCULAR.
(Poster has been cut in center for presentation here.)

distinctive hammer make it easily distinguishable from the larger Vest Pocket.

The prototype of the Vest Pocket .22 came to light in the Remington family collection. In common with other Remington pilot models, it was made largely of bronze. The gun was oversize, in .32 R.F. caliber, rather heavy in construction, with a four-inch octagon barrel. One interesting feature was a steel plate fixed to the breech face of the barrel, to better resist the hammer blow. There were no numbers or markings.

A special light .22 target pistol on a Vest Pocket action was probably one of many Remington "special order" guns. Though our specimen was unmarked except for the serial number "4," appearance and design were unmistakeably Remington. In .22 R.F. short, the gun had a very light ten-inch octagon blued barrel, separate from the action; bead front sight and notch rear; nickel plated built-up receiver; stub trigger adjusted by a set screw, and varnished grips.

VEST POCKET PISTOL .41

Although somewhat similar to the Vest Pocket .22 in general form, this pistol stemmed from Joseph Rider's patent No. 49,887 of December 8, 1863. The arm does have a hammer hung under the barrel and well forward of the breech; but a split breech block is also part of the action. Since the rotating axis of the hammer is forward of that supporting the breech, the movement of cocking allows the breech to be lowered. Once the hammer has fallen to actual firing position, it holds the block in place, and the explosion force is transmitted largely to the hammer pin.

The Vest Pocket .41 sold equally as well as the .22. Remington made a few of the split-breech model in .32 and .38 on special customer and distributor orders.

The prototype of the Vest Pocket .41 (Figure a, Plate XXVII) is in a large mid-West collection. It is slightly bigger than the production gun, and bears a close resemblance to the sketch accompanying Rider's basic patent. Caliber is .38 R.F., barrel is

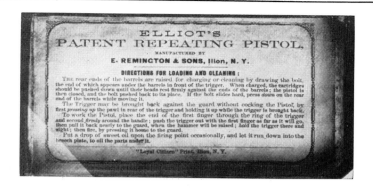

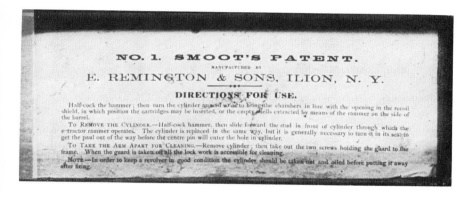

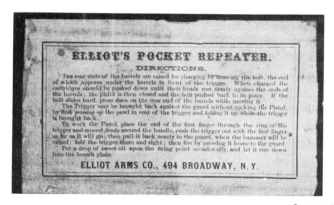

PLATE XXV. GROUP OF OLD REMINGTON INSTRUCTION SHEETS.

4½″ long and overall length is 6¼″. There are no markings or numbers. An outstanding feature of identification is the early form of breech block.

THE ROLLING-BLOCK SYSTEM

Among the first successful breech-loading arms using metallic cartridges, the Model 1865 Navy was one of the first of the Remington single shot rolling-block pistols. All of these used what became known over the world as the "Remington System." Leonard Geiger invented the basic mechanism and protected it by his patent No. 37,501 of January 27, 1863. (Remington learned of that patent, reached Geiger in Europe, whence he had gone to promote his idea, and brought him to Ilion.) Joseph Rider has erroneously been given full credit for the invention and development of this famous action. Rider did contribute to the development—as did several others. Nevertheless, only minor credit is due him, for both his patents cover a fish-hook shaped hammer hung forward of the breech block axis. Even casual examination of the drawings is sufficient to reveal the application of Geiger's patent, a hammer hung back of the breech block axis and supporting the block against the explosion force, to the 1865's and all subsequent models.

THE SINGLE SHOT ROLLING-BLOCK PISTOLS

The patent dates stamped on the left of the receivers originated as follows: (a) May 3, 1864 refers to re-issue 1663 of patent No. 49,887 dated December 8, 1863—Rider; (b) Nov. 15, 1864 refers to patent No. 45,123 of that date—Rider; (c) April 17, 1866 refers to re-issue 2231 of patent No. 37,501 dated January 27, 1863—Geiger.

The action is simple enough to require only a general statement of basic principles. When the hammer is drawn back to full cock, the breech block is held upright by only a light flat spring.

The block can be pulled back for loading, and once the arm is loaded, may be thrown upright again. The piece is then ready to fire. As the hammer descends, its lower portion rolls under the block, wedging the block in place and transmitting the explosion force to the large hammer pin. Changes or improvements are noted under the model in which they appear.

Worthy of representing not only the finest Remington craftsmanship but perhaps the finest American gunmaking, are five companion pieces made for the International Exhibition at Vienna, Austria in 1873. The two cased pairs of pistols in this group are the more remarkable to the Remington collection since "decoration" is not as common with Remington as with other makes and is especially unusual in the truly military models.

The pair shown in Plate XXVIII are made on the 1867 Navy SS pistol action and frame. In approximately .45 caliber, they take a short C.F. bottleneck shell. Barrels are half-octagon with cannon muzzles, bead front sights; grips and fore-ends are ivory; all metal parts are inlaid with silver and gold. The seal of the Royal Austrian House is inlaid in gold on the tops of the receiver rings. "E. Remington & Sons Ilion New York U.S.A." is inlaid in gold on the tops of the barrels. The case contains complete accessories styled to match the guns.

The second cased pair, shown in Plate XXIX (the companion shotgun is not shown) are made on the 1871 Army SS pistol action and frame, in .50 caliber, and take the standard shell. These carry the U. S. eagle, banner and stars in gold inlay on the tops of the receiver rings; the word "Patent" is inlaid in gold on the backstraps; the firm name is inlaid in gold on the tops of the barrels.

Barrels on all five pieces are browned, not blued.

Two Model 1891 Targets have original hooded bead front sights. Another, with open sights, has a silver plated barrel. A third variation of this general model is built on the 1867 Navy action. Except for a V-notch rear sight inlet into the barrel ring, the make-up is "1891."

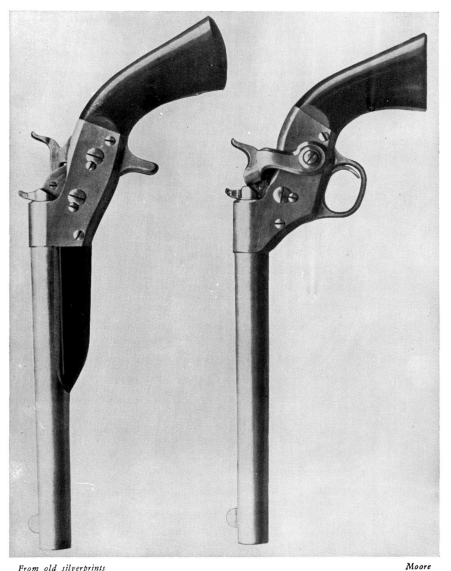

From old silverprints
Courtesy of Mr. C. C. Loomis,

Moore

PLATE XXVI.   PROTOTYPES OF 1865 NAVY AND 1865 ARMY.

MODEL 1865 ARMY

This pistol, illustrative of the general trend of Army thought at the time, will be of interest to arms students. The action, in common with all of the rolling-block "family," is based on Geiger's patent. Instead of a central hammer, one is hung on the outside left of the receiver. The "locking-block" on the inside is separate from the hammer but rotates with it. This model has no firing pin retractor. There are no records to indicate the dates or number manufactured.

MODEL 1865 NAVY

This arm has been the subject of considerable controversy and confusion. Variations in barrel length, finish, and marking, and alterations by both individuals and the Remington Company, have not promoted any clear understanding. Records are not complete, but certain facts unearthed in recent months' research will answer some, at least, of the questions surrounding the 1865.

The heretofore accepted figure of 500 is not anywhere near the total number manufactured. The Navy may or may not have taken only 500. However, as with all Remington service arms, the 1865 Navy was also manufactured for general sale both at home and in foreign countries.

The first models, which went to the Navy, had rim fire breech blocks, stud extractors, no firing pin retractors, and sheath triggers. The barrel was eight and one-half inches long, stamped with an anchor, and in some cases with U.S.N. as well. The 1865's sold to the public may have differed in one or several ways. Following their usual policy, Remington offered to, and did, turn out numbers of these in accordance with particular customer wants. Any of them, however sold, may have been altered later. Specimens have been found with factory installed brass trigger guards or center fire breech blocks or both.

The sheath trigger has been regarded as the salient feature of the 1865 Navy. Actually, Remington would install a sheath

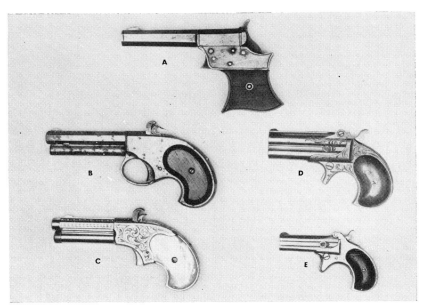

PLATE XXVII.

trigger instead of the triggar guard on any model. In the case of the single shot pistols, the firm offered as late as 1875 in a brochure put out in Spanish the "old model" with trigger guard or sheath trigger in center fire or rim fire. For illustration, the brochure shows an engraving of the 1865 Navy with oval steel trigger guard of the 1867 model. Without doubt, this sales policy explains many of the "non-standard" specimens existing today.

MODEL 1867 NAVY

The 1867 is essentially an improved 1865. A shorter barrel, center fire breech block, and trigger guard are the only changes from the earlier model. Again, variations will be encountered. Sheath triggers, rim fire breech blocks, and odd barrel lengths are not uncommon.

An extension stock (Plate XXX) was tried on the 1867 but, so far as is known, never produced on contract or in numbers. To take the stock, the pistol would have to have been fitted with a grooved butt cap and with studs on the rear of the receiver.

MODEL 1869 TARGET

This target pistol used the 1867 Navy action and grip frame with a seventeen inch full-octagon barrel. A skeleton shoulder stock fitted into a fore and aft groove in the bottom of the flat metal butt cap. These guns, distributed largely by "carpetbag" salesmen, were not regularly listed in factory or agency catalogs.

MODEL 1871 ARMY

The last of the military single shots, this model was, in part, the result of suggestions made by the "St. Louis Commission," an Army Ordnance Board, for improvements on the 1867. A firing pin retractor and rotating extractor were incorporated, the barrel lengthened, the grip modified, and the front sight changed to a long blade. Mainspring force was transmitted to the hammer through a stirrup, instead of by direct contact as in the 1867.

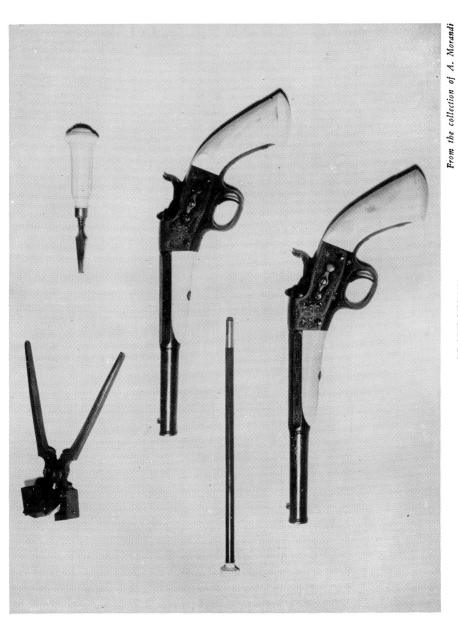

PLATE XXVIII.

MODEL 1879 ARMY

This was a variation of the 1871 action with a sixteen inch half-octagon barrel and a detachable skeleton shoulder stock. Although probably developed on the encouragement of certain Army officials, it apparently never received actual trial. A few were sold to the general public. For illustration see page 54a.

MODEL 1891 TARGET

The action and grips of this target pistol were those of the 1871 Army. A sliding extractor replaced the rotating extractor. A longer half-octagon barrel was the only other change. V-notch rear and blade front sights were standard; grips and fore-ends were smooth.

MODEL 1901 TARGET

This last target pistol was a refinement of the 1891. Sight equipment was Lyman—ivory bead front and adjustable wind gauge rear. Stocks and fore-ends were checkered. The factory guaranteed a uniform trigger pull of three to three and one-half pounds. Standard calibers were .22 short, .22 long rifle, and .44 S. & W. Russian. A variation of the 1901 was put out in .22 long rifle with nine inch round barrel and plain sights as a general purpose or "plinking" pistol.

* * *

Remington licensed firms in Belgium, Spain, and Rumania to manufacture rolling-block pistols. Nagant, in Liege, Belgium, made a double barrel (side by side) pistol for the Russian Government and a single shot for general sale.

In an era of repeating firearms, it was remarkable that one type of single shot pistol should remain on the market for a period of forty-some years. It was also a credit to the Remington brothers' discernment of the possibilities of Geiger's original patent. Even in the last two decades, some target shooters have re-barreled these guns and chambered them for cartridges of moderate pressure—certainly a tribute to the arms designers and gun makers of the nineteenth century.

MASON'S PATENT REVOLVER

William Mason's patent, No. 51,117 dated November 21, 1865, covers a very advanced revolver mechanism. The papers detail a side-swing cartridge revolver featuring simultaneous ejection. The resemblance to a modern Smith and Wesson is close

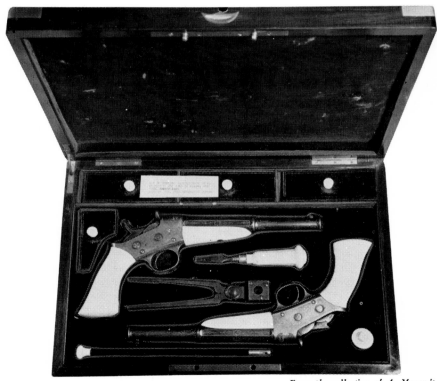

From the collection of A. Morandt

PLATE XXIX.

enough to be startling; crane, starshaped ejector, and front and rear base-pin catches are all there. In this original, however, a knob on the front end of the base pin is pulled forward to release the cylinder. The patent was assigned to E. Remington and Sons. (See Plate XXXI.)

The Mason was manufactured, but in limited numbers. Difficulty in extracting the swelled cases of early rim fire cartridges was, quite possibly, one reason for discontinuing it. Black powder fouling would most certainly have hindered the operation of its closely fitted parts.

No specimen of this revolver has yet turned up for examination. However, other revolvers designed by Mason, using the same principles, and made not too much later, are in existence.

DOUBLE DERRINGER

This derringer is based on William H. Elliot's patent No. 51,440 of December 12, 1865. Two points are claimed: (1) a vertically oscillating firing pin, operated by a cam, for successive discharge; (2) "so constructing and operating the cam and firing pin that they shall serve the purpose of ratchet and pawl." A lever on the right side of the frame unlatches the barrels, which then swing up on a top hinge. The first marketed had no extractor; the later ones were equipped with a long thin hammer spur and a two-armed extractor; the latest and final type had a short hammer spur and a sliding extractor. This design continued as standard until production of the model ceased.

An Illinois collector unearthed a truly massive version of this model some years ago. The gun is nine and one-quarter inches overall, weighs seventeen and one-half ounces, has six inch barrels and chambers a .44 Henry R.F. cartridge. Extraction system is the interim type, though the two arms are now missing. It has the Remington stamp and correct patent date so the origin is unquestioned. A serial number of "2,774" casts at least a shade of doubt on an otherwise sure-fire wager that the gun is a single odd

Moore

PLATE XXX. EXPERIMENTAL SHOULDER STOCK FOR NAVY SINGLE SHOT

special order piece. The armchair guessers may take over. (Plate XXXII.)

Some of the popularity of the Double Derringer, or so we have been told, was due to the ease with which it could be used as a hand bludgeon or "knucks." Grasp the gun by the barrel, and you will grant some credulity to the story.

Figure e, Plate XXVII, shows a miniature edition of the Double Derringer. Caliber is .22 R.F.; barrels are two and one-quarter inches long. Aside from a serial number "1" there are no markings. Workmanship is typically Remington, but the history and purpose of the gun can not be found in any available records. Figure d, adjacent in Plate XXVII shows the conventional size Double Derringer for comparison.

Manufactured over a longer period of time than any other Remington handgun, the Double Derringer records in its markings the course of company affairs. Those made up to 1888 were stamped "E. Remington & Sons"; those made between 1888 and 1910, "Remington Arms Co."; those made between 1910 and 1935, "Remington Arms-U.M.C. Co." In 1935, shortly after Du Pont purchased control of the firm, the Double Derringer was discontinued. It was the last of the Remington pistols and the last of its type on the U.S. market.

ELLIOT SINGLE SHOT DERRINGER

Another patent of prolific Wm. Elliot, No. 68,292 of August 27, 1867, is the basis of this tiny single shot. The mechanism is the acme of simplicity. There are only three principal working parts: hammer, trigger, and mainspring. The firing pin is on the face of the hammer; the hammer in down position functions as breech block.

RIDER MAGAZINE PISTOL

The construction and operation of this pistol are recorded in detail in Rider's patent No. 118,152 dated August 15, 1871. A brief statement of operation is considered adequate here. A maga-

zine is located under the barrel. To load, a spring tube is un-
latched and withdrawn from the magazine housing; cartridges are
placed in the housing; the tube is then re-seated and latched.
When loaded, magazine spring pressure keeps a cartridge always
in the pronged carrier. In preparation for firing, the projection on
the breech block is pressed down, then drawn full back, and released. Backward motion of the block cams the carrier up to a
position behind the chamber and cocks the hammer; forward motion of the block carries a cartridge into the chamber. On successive movements, the spent case is withdrawn by a block-actuated
extractor, and the carrier acts also as an ejector. The slight
vertical motion of the block is due to the fact that it seats itself in
the frame to resist the explosion. Some of these guns were
equipped with a pocket clip somewhat similar to the belt hook
on an old muzzle-loading martial pistol.

The inventor's model (Figure b, Plate XXVII) conforms
closely to the gun pictured in the original patent papers, i.e., it has
a trigger guard. It is larger than the production gun, as you will note
by comparing it with Figure c, adjacent in Plate XXVII. In me-
chanics and operation, the standard arms vary but little from that
of the prototype. The latter is .30 caliber, six and five-eighths
inches overall, and has a three and seven-eighths inch barrel.

NEW LINE REVOLVERS

In 1873 Remington brought out the first of the New Line revolvers, based on William S. Smoot's patent No. 143,855 dated
October 21, 1873. Smoot developed the revolver of that patent
during the months of his provisional connection with Remington.
He came to Ilion in November of 1870, after resigning his Lieu-
tenant's commission in the Ordnance Department of the Army,
and worked there part time until April of 1871. He was then engaged full time, later became superintendent of the manufacturing department, and finally a trustee of the company. His connection with the firm ended in 1885.

From a strictly shooter's standpoint, there is nothing particu-

W. MASON.
REVOLVING FIREARM.

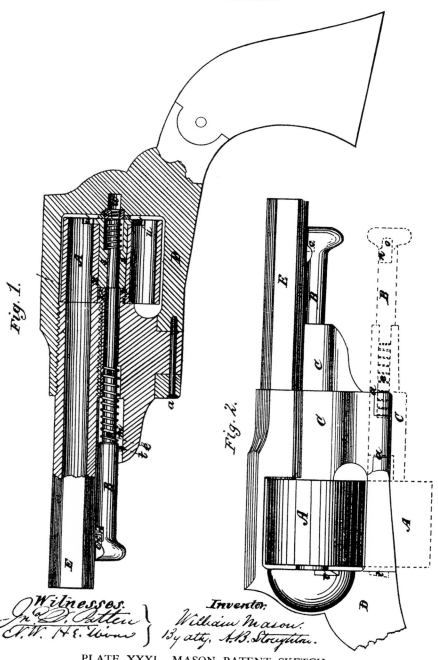

Fig. 1.

Fig. 2.

Witnesses.

Jno. D. Patten

N. W. H. E. Winn

Inventor:

William Mason.

By atty, A. B. Stoughton.

PLATE XXXI. MASON PATENT SKETCH

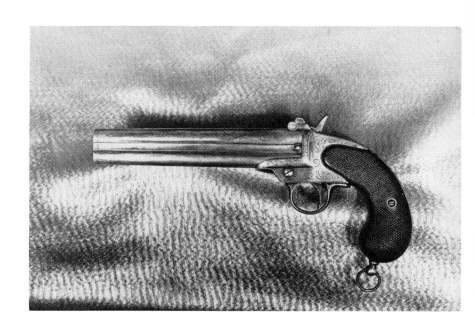

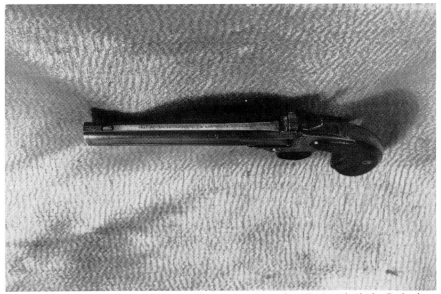

PLATE XXXII.

larly novel in the appearance or operation of the New Line revolvers. Any manufacturer would note the parts breakdown and
method of assembly with definite interest. The patent papers give
a very good description of the early Smoots:

> The invention consists in a peculiar manner of forming the barrel and
> frame of a single piece of metal in connection with the guard strap; in a
> revolving recoil-shield of novel construction; a novel construction and
> arrangement of the ejector and center-pin. . . .
> In constructing my revolver, I make the barrel and the frame, with the
> bridge or strap that connects them above the cylinder, all in one piece of
> metal, the rear end of the frame extending back far enough to form the
> upper portion of the handle, the guard strap, made also of a single piece,
> forming the lower portion of the handle and frame, the two parts being
> united by [screws, front and rear] the hammer being pivoted in the
> [upper] part, and the trigger and stop, with their springs . . . in the
> lower part . . . this mode of construction affording great convenience
> of manufacture, and also affording convenient access to the lock.

The ejector spring housing is integral with the barrel, and
underneath it. The base pin enters the rear end of the passage
containing the ejector spring. This feature makes both the ejector
and base pin spring-loaded. The ejector may be drawn to the
rear or the base pin forward, for ejection or cylinder removal
respectively. The revolving recoil shield has a side opening, which
may be presented or concealed.

NEW LINE No. 1

The No. 1, in .30 rim fire short, has the integral frame and
barrel of Smoot's patent. Those first made have also the revolving
recoil shield; those made later have a solid shield. Although the
revolver was designed, manufactured, and advertised as a cartridge
gun, a few must have been made with percussion cylinder on special order. Parts lists from 1879 to 1882 include "cone cylinders"
and "cones" for the Smoot No. 1.

NEW LINE No. 2

This model is .32 rim fire short. In every other respect, it is
identical with the No. 1. As with the .30 caliber, the first made
have the revolving recoil shield; later ones, the solid shield.

NEW LINE No. 3

Standard caliber was .38 rim fire short, but specimens in .38 center fire have been noted. In this number, Remington departed from the original patent and fabricated the barrel separately. Two styles were made: one had a top-ribbed octagon barrel (as in the No. 1 and 2) and modified saw handle grip; the other had an un-ribbed octagon barrel and bird head grip. Both had a solid recoil shield.

NEW LINE No. 4

Although retaining the Smoot lock and frame parting-line, this model departed even further from the original design. The short round barrel was fabricated separately. No ejector was pro-vided, so the design allowed utilization of a simple base pin with knurled head. Calibers were .38 or .41 rim fire short, .38 center fire, and .41 center fire short.

MODEL 1875

Originally, the Model 1875 was chambered for the .44 Rem-ington C. F. cartridge. References indicate that the .44 Colt should chamber in revolvers made for the .44 Rem. Actually, the Colt round will not do so unless, from the many variations in case diameter, one could select a lot manufactured to absolute minimum dimensions. We can testify to the fact that the tight chambers of the early production 1875's will not accept an aver-age .44 Colt round. With guns numbered "24" and "57" a .44 Rem. cartridge slips in to a snug fit; a .44 Colt will seat only to about two-thirds the case length. About 1879 the arm was also offered for sale in .45 Gov. and .44 W. C. F.

The 1875's generally encountered are equipped with lanyard loops, oil finished walnut grips and either of two types of fixed front sights. One type is the common blade front, and the other is a small iron sight a la New Model .44 percussion. Custom built guns have been found with short (5½ inch) barrels, without lanyard loops, with brass or German silver blade front sights, with engraving, or special finish or grips.

At various times Remington designated this the Egyptian model, and Improved Army, and the No. 3 Army (the percussion .44 was known as No. 1, the conversion as No. 2). Ten thousand of these went to the Egyptian Government in 1875. Our original data indicated that a quantity of these revolvers were purchased by the U. S. Government. As the years have passed, and more contemporary documents have come to light, serious doubts have arisen as to whether any such official purchase of this arm was ever made. Also, to the best of our knowledge, no specimens have ever appeared with authentic "US" markings. The *alleged* number purchased remains in the data table, with a question mark—it points to the controversy that has surrounded this revolver from its very inception.

In reference to the .44 Rem. pistol cartridge itself, the round seems to have been limited to small production and a short life on the market, expiring by or before 1888.

IROQUOIS REVOLVER

In outside appearance this little .22 bears a marked resemblance to the New Line No. 4's. The construction and lock parts are quite different. It has a solid frame; on the left rear, adjacent to the hammer, is a removable circular plate. By taking out the plate, a round hand spring can be removed. Other than this peculiar small spring, the lock is a simple single action type of conventional design.

When first brought out, the Iroquois was advertised with plain or fluted cylinder and designated No. 1 and No. 2 respectively. Not all the early models were stamped "Iroquois."

Many of these have appeared without any markings.

MODEL 1890

This was actually the 1875 with the web under the barrel cut away. It was made in two barrel lengths, five and one-half and seven and one-half inches, but only one caliber—.44-40. Like its

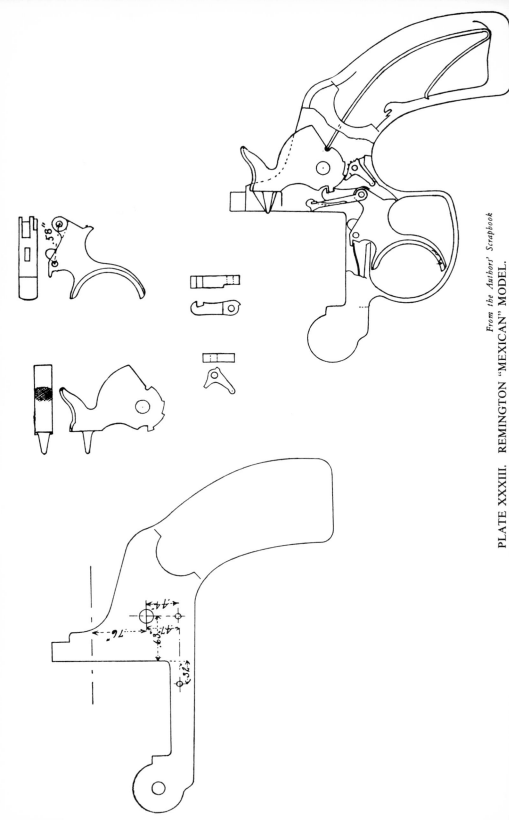

PLATE XXXIII. REMINGTON "MEXICAN" MODEL.

From the Authors' Scrapbook

predecessors, this arm was called the Improved Army in advertising literature.

MODEL 1891 TIP-UP (MEXICAN)

This double action top-break revolver, .38 center fire, five shot, with bronze frame, was made for the Mexican Government. The parts and assembly were being designed in 1891; the contract, estimated at 2,000, was completed by or before 1895. No complete assembly drawing or specimen could be obtained for reproduction. Enough component parts and drawings have been seen to authenticate its manufacture.

MODEL 51 AUTOMATIC PISTOL

The "51" can be described briefly as a hammerless, locked-breech, side-ejecting pocket automatic. The basic patent, No. 1,348,733 dated August 3, 1920, was issued to John D. Pedersen, one of the ablest of modern firearms designers. The original application for patent was filed July 30, 1915 and renewed July 17, 1919. Seven other patents issued on various features of this arm, six to Pedersen and one to Crawford C. Loomis, were finally granted in 1920.

Three safeties were incorporated: grip, thumb, and magazine. The grip safety must be depressed before firing; it also acts as an indicator, since it stays seated when the piece is not cocked. The thumb safety functions as an indicator of hammer position, since it cannot be thrown "safe" unless the arm is ready to fire. Thirdly, the gun will not fire if the magazine has been withdrawn.

A remarkable amount of development work was done on this model before it ever reached the sales counter. Several features command attention even today. The grip form was the result of intensive study on what shape best fitted the average hand. The angle of the grip with the barrel was designed to provide effortless pointing. The extreme top of the slide was flat, and matted to prevent light reflection. Sights were low, and square for quick accurate shooting. Considerably more than idle wonder can be given to the reasons other arms makers took so long to follow Remington's lead in hand guns. The much heralded advent of "guns fitted to the shooter" takes on a slightly brassy luster when held up beside the Model 51 Automatic (circa 1915).

A .45 caliber version of the "51" was made for the Government small arms tests in 1919. Although the arm performed well and found favor with the Navy, considerations of inter-service standardization prevented its adoption. None were manufactured for commercial sale.

Markings on this gun given in the catalog section (page 133) were those on an early production gun. Markings on a very late arm are as follows:

On slide: "Remington Arms Company, Inc. Ilion, N. Y., U.S.A. Pedersen Patents Pat'd Mar. 9, 20, Aug. 3, 20, Oct 12, 20, June 14, 21, Others Pending"

On chamber (ejection port): ".32 Cal 7.65 MM"

Trigger guard: Anchor on right side, "PT" on left

Serial No.: PA 69094

*   *   *

During the First World War Remington manufactured the .45 Government Automatic and the U.S. Mark 111 Signal Pistol. Another "arm" manufactured toward the close of that war deserves mention here by reason of its title. The "Automatic Pistol, Caliber .30, Model 1918," was actually an attachment to be used in place of the bolt in a Springfield rifle to provide semi-automatic fire. The attachment, known also as the "Pedersen Device" after its inventor, J. D. Pedersen, took a forty-shot magazine inserted at the top right. The outside muzzle end of the barrel was identical in shape to a .30-'06 cartridge case so that it fitted into the regular chamber. The device was given its title "pistol" for security reasons.

6 ■ ■

CATALOG OF
CARTRIDGE MODELS

THE MODEL designations are, in most cases, those originally given the arms by the Remington Company. Where Remington used several titles for the same arm, the authors have tried to choose the most accurate and descriptive. Where the Remington title was vague or applied to several arms, the authors have adopted the designation generally accepted by collectors.

Years of manufacture were determined on the basis of patent dates stamped on arms, known sales and contracts, and Remington catalogs and advertisements. Estimates of the number manufactured of the various models are based on known contracts and sales, known statements of the company in the past, probable rates of production, and known serial numbers. These estimates were arrived at by the authors in collaboration with Mr. Loomis. Since none of the material used in making these estimates is the property of the Remington Arms Company, although much of it was made available through their co-operation, they understandably do not wish to be held officially responsible for the accuracy of the figures.

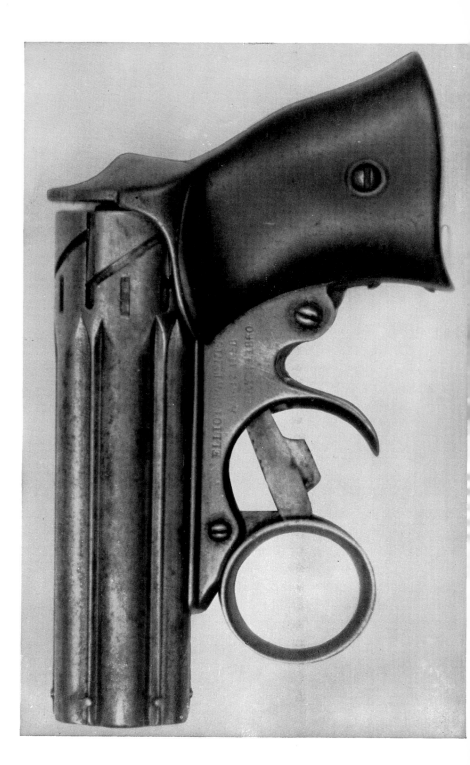

PLATE XXXIV.
ZIG-ZAG DERRINGER
(Double Action)

Distinctive feature: grooves on rear of barrel cluster
Markings—
  Left side of frame: ELLIOT'S PATENT AUG. 17, 1858
    MAY 29, 1860
  Right side of frame: MANUFACTURED BY REMING-
    TON'S, ILION, N. Y.
Serial number: side of grip frame
Dates of manufacture: 1861-1862
Number manufactured: estimated at less than 1,000

Caliber: .22
Number of shots: 6
Barrels: 3 3/16", fluted, with rib in each flute
Rifling: 5 grooves
Trigger: ring
Sights: front, brass pin each flute; *rear,* groove
Grips: hard rubber, smooth
Finish: blued
Weight: 8 ounces

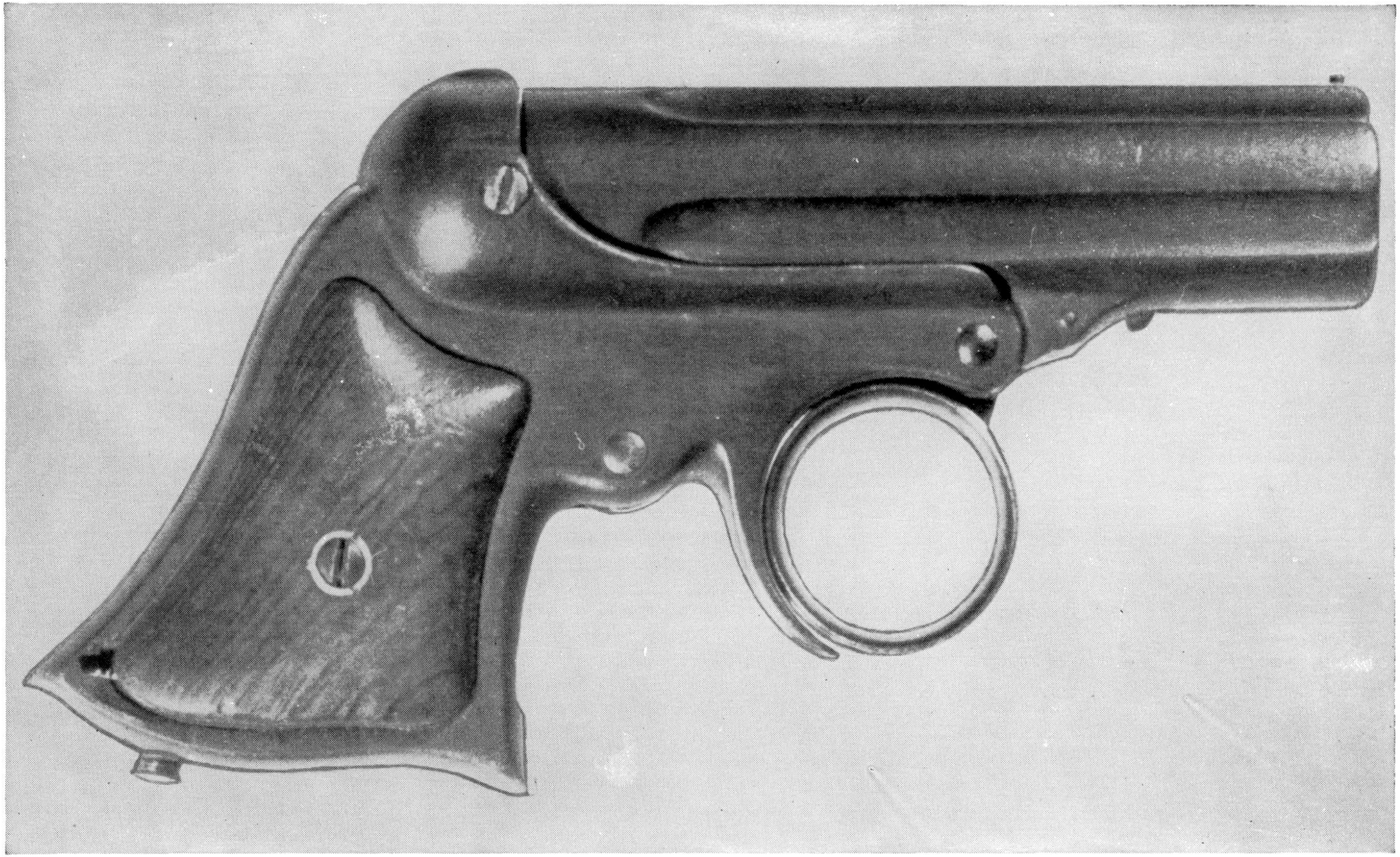

From the collection of Mr. C. C. Loomis, of Lion, New York

PLATE XXXV.
REMINGTON-ELLIOTT DERRINGER
(Double Action)

Caliber: .22 rim fire
Number of shots: 5
Barrel: 3", round cluster, fluted
Rifling: 5 grooves
Trigger: ring
Sights: front, brass pin; rear, groove
Grips: hard rubber, smooth; pearl; ivory
Finish: blued; nickel plated frame; full nickel plated; specially
  plated or engraved on order

Weight: 8½ ounces
Markings—
  Left side of barrel: MANUFACTURED BY E. REMING-
    TON & SONS, ILION, N. Y.
  Right side of barrel: ELLIOT'S PATENTS MAY 29, 1860-
    OCT. 1, 1861
Serial number: inside frame; side of grip frame
Dates of manufacture: 1863-1888
Number manufactured: estimated at over 50,000 for caliber
  .22 and .32 together

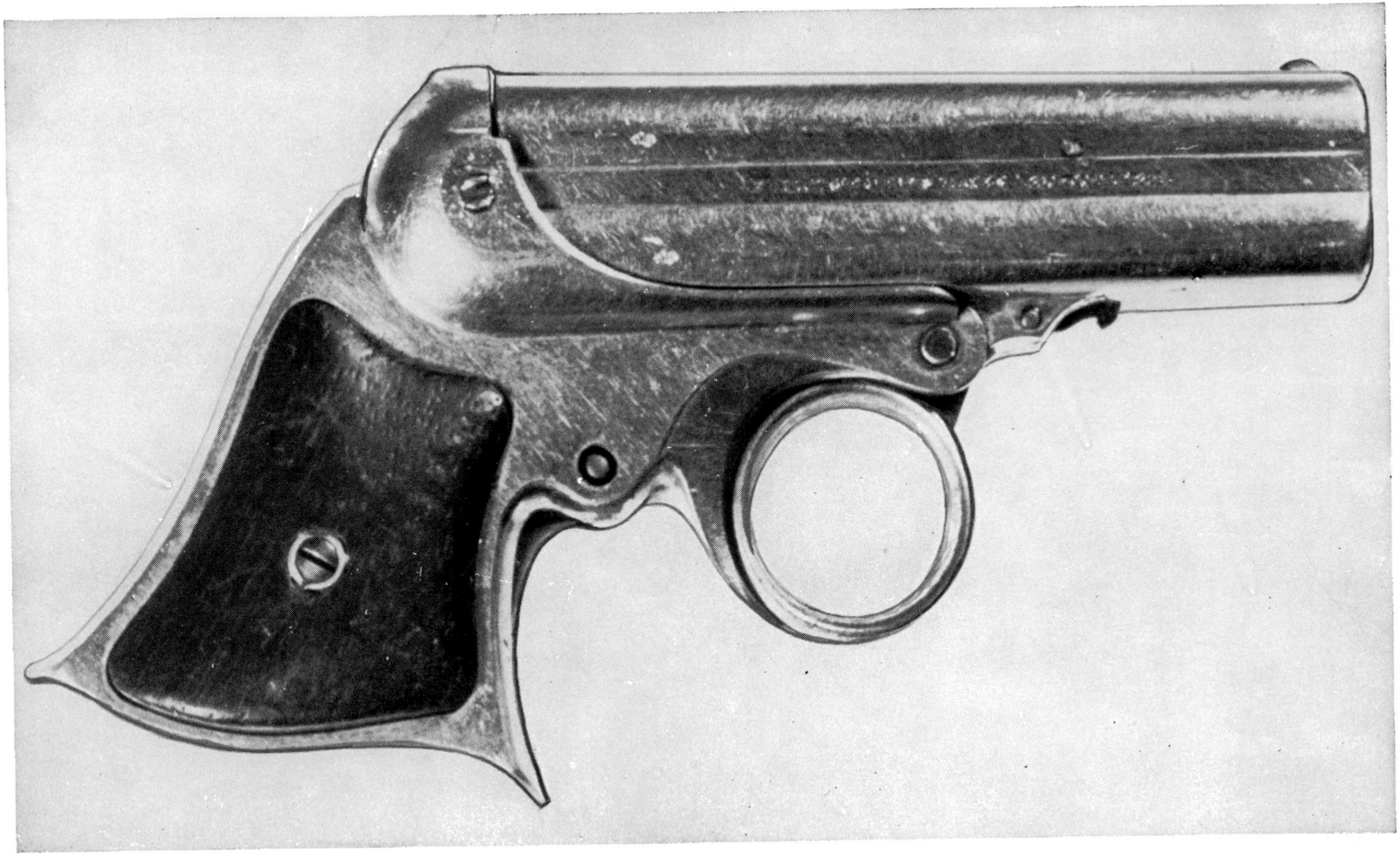

From the collection of Mr. C. C. Loomis, of Lion, New York

PLATE XXXVI.
REMINGTON-ELLIOTT DERRINGER
(Double Action)

Caliber: .32 rim fire
Number of shots: 4
Barrel: 3⅜", square cluster, fluted
Rifling: 5 grooves
Trigger: ring
Sights: front, brass blade; *rear,* groove
Grips: hard rubber, smooth; pearl; ivory
Finish: blued; nickel planted frame; full nickel plated; especially plated or engraved on order

Weight: 13 ounces
Markings—
  Left side of barrel: MANUFACTURED BY E. REMINGTON & SON, ILION, N. Y.
  Right side of barrel: ELLIOT'S PATENTS MAY 29, 1860-OCT. 1, 1861
Serial number: inside frame; side of grip frame
Dates of manufacture: 1863-1888
Number manufactured: estimated at over 50,000 for caliber .22 and .32 together

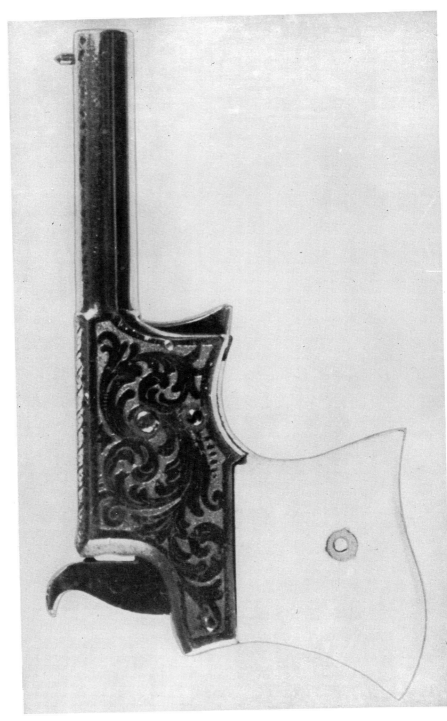

PLATE XXXVII.
VEST POCKET PISTOL—.22
(Single Action)

Caliber: .22 rim fire
Number of shots: 1
Barrel: 3¼" round
Rifling: 5 grooves
Trigger: sheath
Sights: front, brass pin; rear, groove
Grips: walnut, varnished; pearl; ivory

Finish: blued; plated; engraving on order
Weight: 3⅞ ounces
Markings—
  Top of barrel: REMINGTON'S, ILION, N. Y. PATENT
    OCT. 1, 1861
Serial number: underside of barrel; side of grip frame
Dates of manufacture: 1865-1888
Number manufactured: estimated at over 25,000

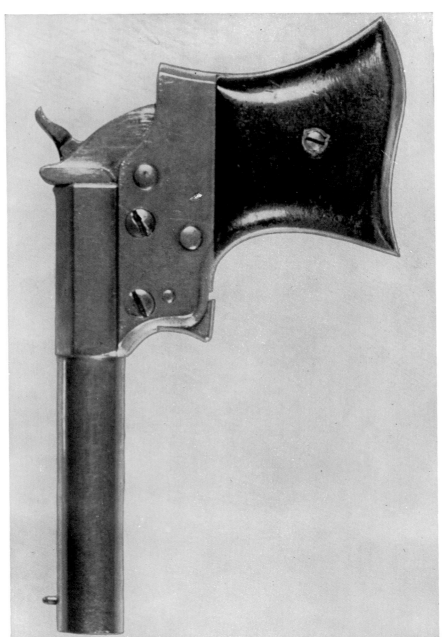

Moore

PLATE XXXVIII.
VEST POCKET PISTOL—.41
(Single Action)

Caliber: .41
Number of shots: 1
Barrel: 4" octagon round
Rifling: 5 grooves
Trigger: sheath
Sights: front, brass pin, *rear,* groove
Grips: walnut, varnished; pearl; ivory

Finish: blued; nickel plated frame; full nickel plated; specially
plated or engraved on order
Weight: 11 ounces
Markings—
Top of barrel: REMINGTON'S ILION, N. Y. PAT. OCT.
1, 1861-NOV. 15, 1864
Serial number: underside of barrel; side of grip frame
Dates of manufacture: 1865-1888
Number manufactured: estimated at over 25,000

Moore

From the authors' collection

PLATE XXXIX.
MODEL 1865 NAVY
(Single Action)

Caliber: .50 rim fire
Number of shots: 1
Barrel: 8½" round
Rifling: 3 grooves
Trigger: sheath
Sights: front, iron blade; rear, V-notch in breech block
Grips: walnut, oil finished
Finish: blued barrel, case-hardened receiver, breech block, hammer, trigger, and sheath; some barrels and receivers tinned

Weight: 2 pounds, 4 ounces
Markings—
   Top of barrel: anchor
   Left side of receiver: REMINGTON ILION, N. Y. U.S.A. PAT. MAY 3d NOV. 15th, 1864, APRIL 17th, 1866
   Right side of receiver: P FCW (not on all specimens)
   Left grip: inspector's initials in script in medallion
Serial number: side of grip frame
Dates of manufacture: 1866-1875
Number manufactured: estimated at well over 1,000

PLATE XL.
MODEL 1867 NAVY
(Single Action)

Caliber: .50 center fire
Number of shots: 1
Barrel: 7" round
Rifling: 3 grooves
Trigger: guard; iron, oval
Sights: front, iron blade; rear, V-notch in breech block
Grips: walnut, oil finished
Finish: blued barrel, case-hardened receiver, breech block, hammer, trigger, and trigger guard

Weight: 2 pounds
Markings—
  Top of barrel: I/W.D.W./anchor
  Left side of receiver: REMINGTON'S ILION, N. Y. U.S.A.
    PAT. MAY 3d NOV. 15th 1864 APRIL 17th, 1866
  Right side of receiver: P FCW
  Left grip: inspector's initials in script in medallion
Serial number: underside of barrel; side of grip frame
Dates of manufacture: 1867-1875
Number manufactured: over 7,000

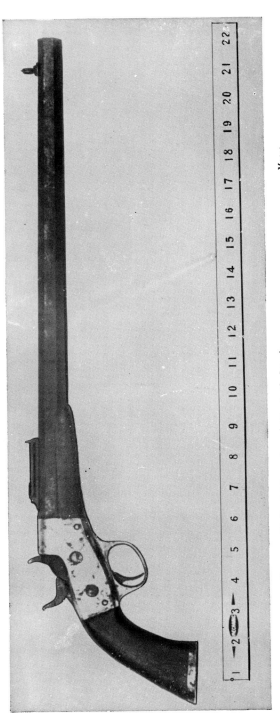

From an old silverprint, courtesy of Mr. C. C. Loomis

Moore

PLATE XLI.
MODEL 1869 TARGET
(Single Action)

Caliber: .22
Number of shots: 1
Barrel: 17" octagon
Rifling: 5 grooves
Trigger guard: iron, oval
Sights: front, globe; *rear,* buckhorn
Grips: walnut, varnished

Finish: blued
Weight: not known
Markings—
    Not known
Dates of manufacture: 1869-1888
Number manufactured: no record

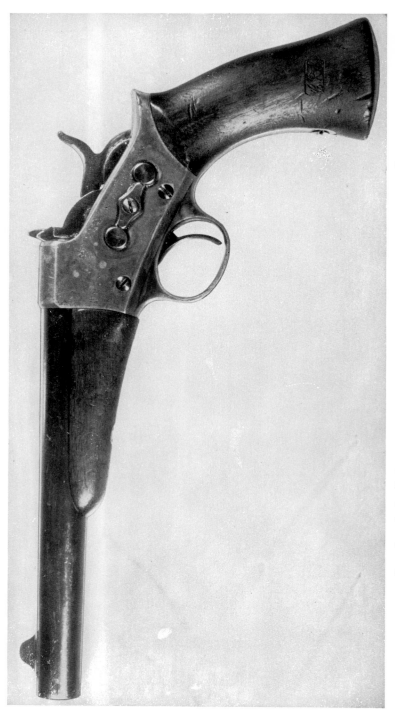

Moore

PLATE XLII.
MODEL 1871 ARMY
(Single Action)

Caliber: .50 center fire
Number of shots: 1
Barrel: 8" round
Rifling: 3 grooves
Trigger guard: iron, oval
Sights: front, large iron blade; *rear,* V-notch in breech block
Grips: walnut, oil finished

Finish: blued barrel, trigger; case-hardened receiver, trigger
    guard; bright hammer, breech block
Weight: 2 pounds, 3 ounces
Markings—
    Left side of receiver: REMINGTONS ILION, N. Y. U.S.A.
    PAT. MAY 3d NOV. 15th, 1864 APRIL 17th, 1866 P S
Serial number: side of grip frame
Dates of manufacture: 1872-1888
Number manufactured: over 6,000

Moore

From the authors' collection

PLATE XLIII.
MODEL 1891 TARGET
(Single Action)

Caliber: .22 rim fire, .25 rim fire, .32-20, .32 S.&W. rim fire (short or long) .32 S.&W. center fire

Barrel: 10" half-octagon (8" and 12" barrel lengths have been noted)

Rifling: 5 grooves

Number of shots: 1

Trigger guard: iron, oval

Sights: front, German silver blade; *rear,* adjustable V-notch (Rocky Mountain)

Grips: walnut, oil finished

Finish: blued barrel, breech block, trigger; case-hardened receiver, trigger guard; bright hammer

Weight: 2 pounds, 13 ounces (in .22 caliber)

Markings—

   Top of barrel: REMINGTON ARMS CO. ILION, N. Y.

   Left side of receiver: REMINGTON'S ILION, N. Y. U.S.A. PAT. MAY 3d NOV. 15th 1864 APRIL 17th 1866 P S

   Left grip: inspector's initials in script in medallion

Serial number: side of grip frame

Dates of manufacture: 1891-1900

Number manufactured: approximately 100

REMINGTON . FIREARMS

Remington Single-Shot Target Pistol

NEW MODEL

FOR TARGET AND GALLERY PRACTICE

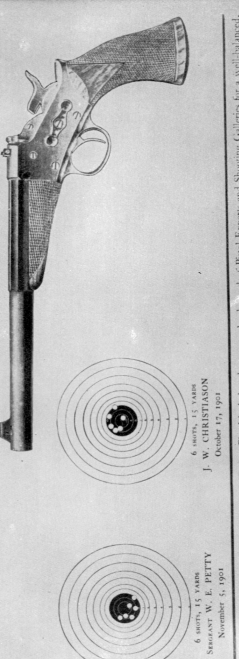

6 SHOTS, 15 YARDS
SERGEANT W. E. PETTY
November 5, 1901

6 SHOTS, 15 YARDS
J. W. CHRISTIASON
October 17, 1901

The Remington New Model Target Pistol is designed to meet the demand of Pistol Experts and Shooting Galleries for a well-balanced, accurate, and finely adjusted arm. The breech mechanism is the well-known "Remington" system, combining simplicity, convenience and durability. Half-octagon, 10-inch barrel, carefully bored, rifled and finished. Stock and tip selected walnut, finely checkered. Ivory bead front sight; adjustable wind-gauge rear sight. Mechanism finely finished to insure uniform trigger pull of 3 to 3½ lbs. Weight, 2½ lbs. . . . . $16 00.

22 Short rim-fire, 22 Long Rifle rim-fire, 44 S. & W. Russian central-fire.

From the 1902 Remington Catalog

PLATE XLIV.
MODEL 1901 TARGET
(Single Action)

Caliber: .22 long rifle, .22 rim fire short, .25-10 rim fire, .44
    S.&W. Russian
Barrel: 10" half-octagon
Rifling: 5 grooves
Number of shots: 1
Trigger guard: iron, oval
Sights: front, ivory bead; *rear,* adjustable wind gauge
Grips: walnut, checkered
Forearm: walnut, checkered
Finish: blued
Weight: 2 pounds, 13 ounces (in .22 caliber)
Markings—
    Top of barrel: REMINGTON ARMS CO. ILION, N. Y.
    Left side of receiver: REMINGTON'S ILION, N. Y. U.S.A.
        PAT. MAY 3d NOV. 15th 1864 APRIL 17th 1866
Serial number: side of grip frame
Dates of manufacture: 1901-1909
Number manufactured: approximately 700

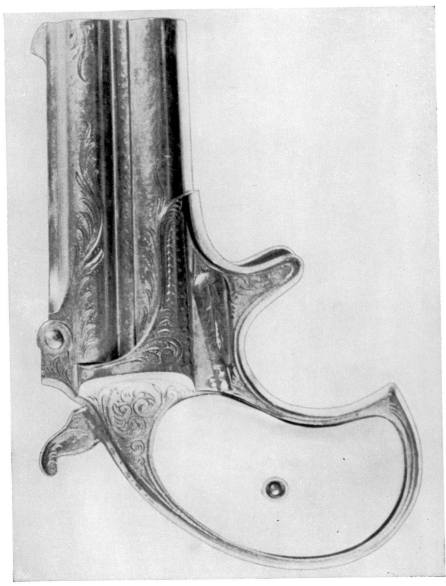

Moore

PLATE XLV.
DOUBLE DERRINGER
(Single Action)

Caliber: .41 rim fire
Number of shots: 2
Barrels: 3" round, superposed
Rifling: 5 grooves
Trigger: sheath
Sights: front, steel blade, integral; *rear,* groove
Grips: walnut, varnished; hard rubber, checkered; pearl; ivory
Finish: blued; nickel plated frame; full nickel plated; specially plated or engraved on order
Weight: 11 ounces
Markings—
   Top of barrel: E. REMINGTON & SONS ILION N. Y. ELLIOTS PATENT DEC. 12th 1865 or REMINGTON ARMS CO. ILION N. Y. or REMINGTON ARMS-U. M. C. CO. ILION N. Y.
Serial number: inside frame; side of grip frame
Dates of manufacture: 1866-1935
Number manufactured: estimated at over 150,000
Note: Some marked on side-rib instead of top of barrel.

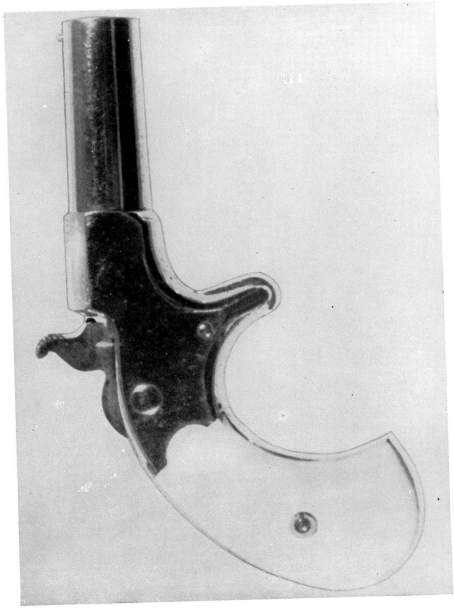

Moore

From the Remington Museum

PLATE XLVI.
ELLIOT SINGLE SHOT DERRINGER
(Single Action)

Caliber: .41 rim fire
Barrel: 2½" round
Rifling: 5 grooves
Trigger: sheath
Sights: front, brass pin
Grips: walnut, varnished; pearl; ivory
Finish: blued; nickel plated frame; full nickel plated
Weight: 7 ounces

Markings—
  Top of barrel: REMINGTONS, ILION, N. Y. ELLIOT
    PAT. AUG. 27, 1867
  Serial number: underside of barrel; underside of receiver
  Dates of manufacture: 1867-1888
  Number manufactured: estimated at 10,000

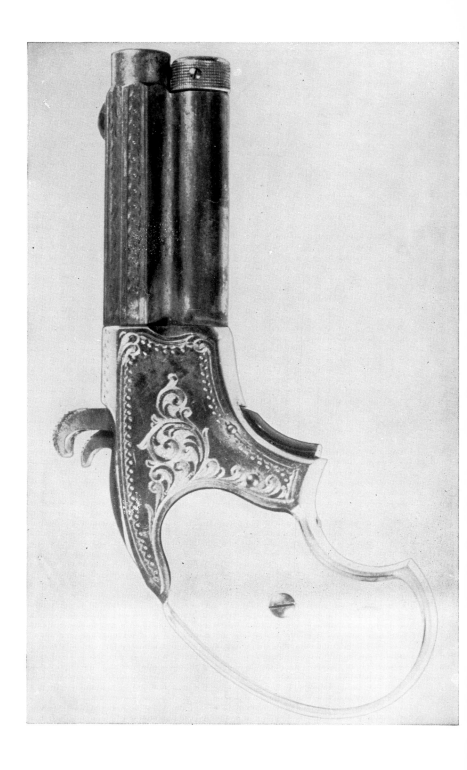

PLATE XLVII.
RIDER MAGAZINE PISTOL
(Single Action)

Caliber: .32 rim fire extra short
Number of shots: 5 in magazine
Barrel: 3″ octagon
Rifling: 5 grooves
Trigger: sheath
Sights: front, brass blade
Grips: walnut, varnished; pearl; ivory

Finish: nickel plated; case-hardened; specially plated or engraved on order
Weight: 10 ounces
Markings—
    Top of barrel: E. REMINGTON & SONS, ILION, N. Y.
        RIDERS PAT. AUG. 15, 1871
Serial number: side of grip frame
Dates of manufacture: 1871-1888
Number manufactured: estimated at 15,000

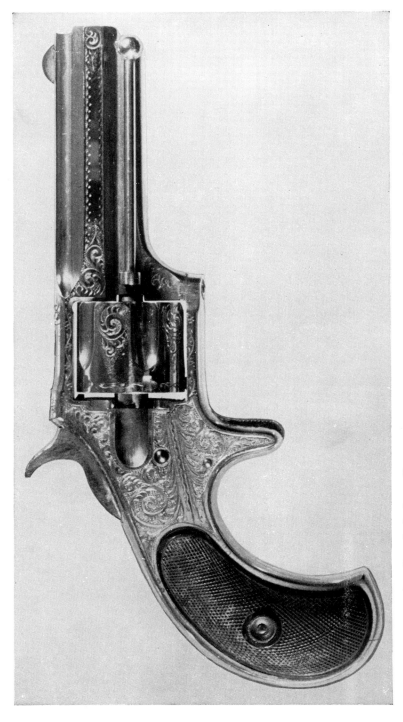

Moore

PLATE XLVIII.
NEW LINE REVOLVER, NO. 1
(Single Action)

Caliber: .30 rim fire short
Number of shots: 5
Barrel: 2 13/16" octagon
Rifling: 5 grooves
Cylinder: 13/16" long
Trigger: sheath
Sights: front, blade: rear, groove
Grips: walnut, varnished; hard rubber, checkered; pearl; ivory

Finish: blued; nickel plated; specially plated or engraved on
    order
Weight: 10 ounces
Distinctive feature: unique rod ejector
Markings—
    Top of barrel: E. REMINGTON & SONS, ILION, N. Y.
    PAT. W. S. SMOOT OCT. 21, 1873
Serial number: side of grip frame
Dates of manufacture: 1873-1888
Number manufactured: estimated at over 20,000

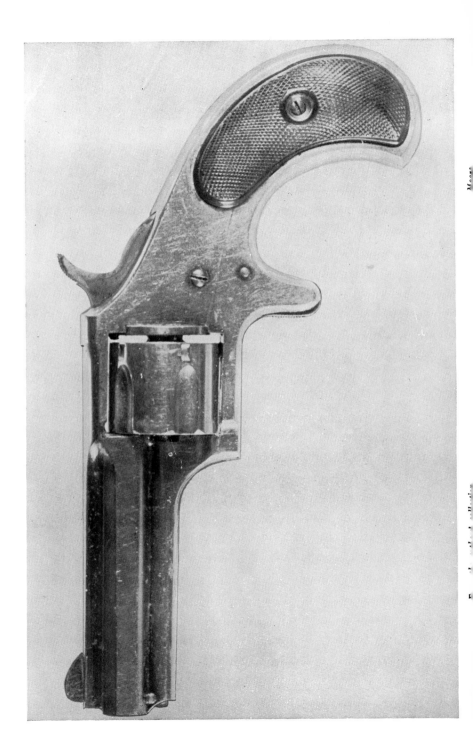

PLATE XLIX.
NEW LINE REVOLVER, NO. 2
(Single Action)

Caliber: .32 rim fire short
Number of shots: 5
Barrel: 2¾" octagon
Rifling: 5 grooves
Cylinder: ⅞" long
Trigger: sheath
Sights: front, blade; *rear,* groove
Grips: hard rubber; checkered; pearl; ivory

Finish: blued; nickel plated; specially plated or engraved on order
Weight: 10 ounces
Distinctive feature: unique rod ejector
Markings—
   Top of barrel: E. REMINGTON & SONS, ILION, N. Y.
      PAT. W. S. SMOOT OCT. 21, 1873
Serial number: side of grip frame
Dates of manufacture: 1874-1888
Number manufactured: estimated at over 20,000

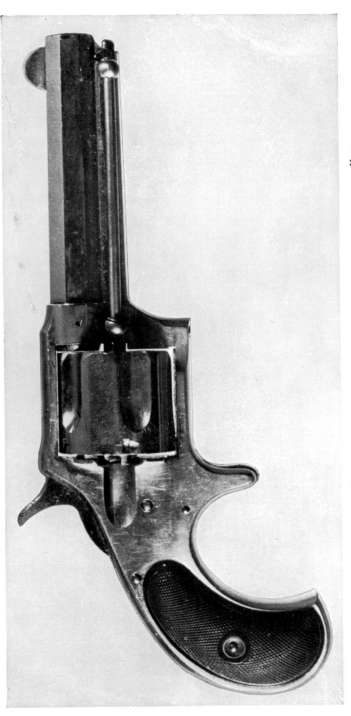

PLATE L.
NEW LINE REVOLVER, NO. 3
(Single Action)

Caliber: .38 rim fire short
Number of shots: 5
Barrel: 3¾" octagon
Rifling: 5 grooves
Cylinder: 1 3/16" long
Trigger: sheath
Sights: front, blade; *rear,* groove
Grips: hard rubber, checkered; pearl; ivory
Finish: blued; nickel plated; specially plated or engraved on
order

Weight: 15 ounces
Distinctive feature: unique rod ejector
Markings—
   Top of barrel: E. REMINGTON & SONS, ILION, N. Y.
     PAT. W. S. SMOOT OCT. 21, 1873
Serial number: side of grip frame
Dates of manufacture: 1875-1888
Number manufactured: estimated at over 25,000 for both types

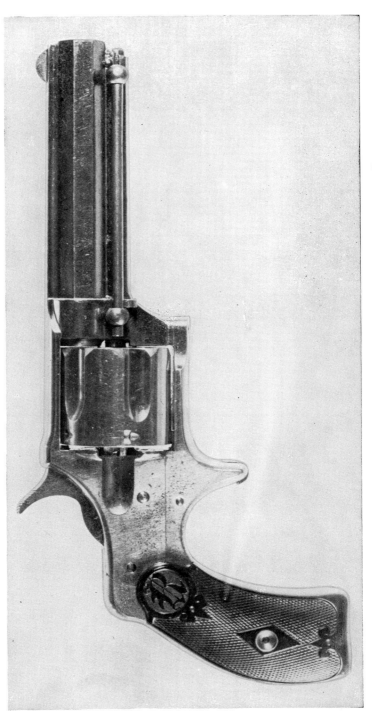

Moore

From the authors' collection

PLATE LI.
NEW LINE REVOLVER NO. 3
(Single Action)

Caliber: .38 center fire, .38 rim fire short
Number of shots: 5
Barrel: 3¾″ octagon
Rifling: 5 grooves
Cylinder: 1 3/16″ long
Trigger: sheath
Sights: front, blade; *rear,* groove
Grips: hard rubber, checkered; pearl; ivory
Finish: blued; nickel plated; specially plated or engraved on
    order
Weight: 15 ounces
Distinctive features: unique rod ejector
Markings—
    Top of barrel: E. REMINGTON & SONS, ILION, N. Y.
        PAT. W. S. SMOOT OCT. 21, 1873
Serial number: side of grip frame
Dates of manufacture: 1875-1888
Number manufactured: estimated at over 25,000 for both types

PLATE LII.
NEW LINE REVOLVER, NO. 4
(Single Action)

Caliber: .38 center fire short, .41 rim fire short
Number of shots: 5
Barrel: 2½" round
Rifling: 5 grooves
Cylinder: 1 1/16" long
Trigger: sheath
Sights: front, blade; *rear,* groove
Grips: hard rubber; checkered; pearl; ivory
Finish: blued; nickel plated; specially plated or engraved on
order
Weight: 12 ounces
Distinctive feature: no ejector
Markings—
Top of barrel: E. REMINGTON & SONS, ILION, N. Y.
Serial number: inside top strap; side of grip frame
Dates of manufacture: 1877-1888
Number manufactured: estimated at over 10,000

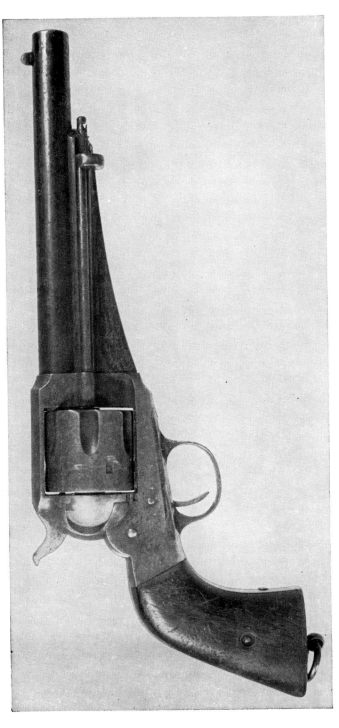

PLATE LIII.
MODEL 1875 ARMY REVOLVER
(Single Action)

Caliber: .44 Rem. center fire; .44-40; .45 Govt.
Number of shots: 6
Barrel: 7½" round
Rifling: 5 grooves
Cylinder: 1 17/32" long
Trigger guard: iron, oval
Sights: front, German silver blade; rear, groove
Grips: walnut, oil finished
Finish: blued, except case-hardened hammer, loading gate
Weight: 2 pounds, 12 ounces
Distinctive features: rod ejector; lanyard loop

Markings—
Top of barrel: E. REMINGTON & SONS, ILION, N. Y. U.S.A.
Left grip: inspector's initials
Serial number: inside top strap; side of grip frame
Dates of manufacture: 1875-1889
Number manufactured: estimated at 25,000
Note: Model 1875's sold to the general public were usually nickel plated. Specially plated or engraved pieces with pearl or ivory grips could be had at extra cost.

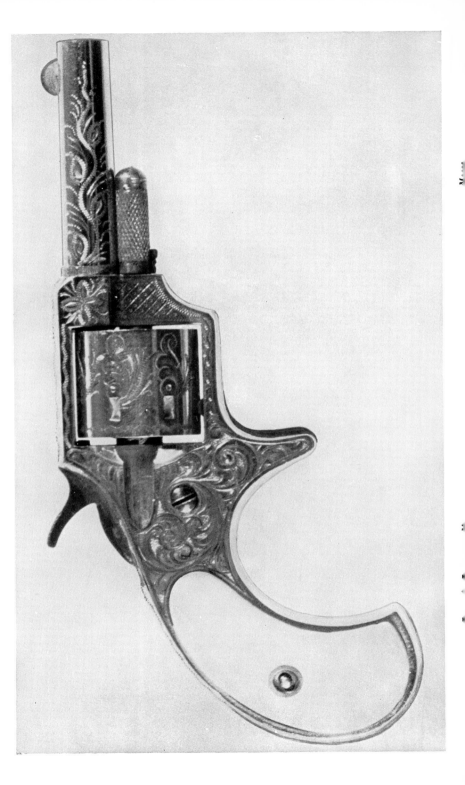

PLATE LIV.
IROQUOIS REVOLVER
(Single Action)

Caliber: .22
Number of shots: 7
Barrel: 2¼" round
Rifling: 5 grooves
Cylinder: 27/32" long
Trigger: sheath
Sights: front, blade; rear, groove
Grips: hard rubber, checkered; pearl; ivory
Finish: blued, nickel plated; specially plated or engraved on order
Weight: 7½ ounces
Distinctive feature: no ejector
Markings—
    Top of barrel: IROQUOIS
    Side of barrel: REMINGTON, ILION, N. Y.
Serial number: side of grip frame
Dates of manufacture: 1878-1888
Number manufactured: estimated at 50,000

PLATE LV.
MODEL 1890 ARMY REVOLVER
(Single Action)

Caliber: .44-40
Number of shots: 6
Barrel: 5½", 7½" round
Rifling: 5 grooves
Cylinder: 17/32" long
Trigger guard: iron, oval
Sights: front, blade; *rear,* groove
Grips: hard rubber, checkered; pearl; ivory

Finish: blued; nickel plated; specially plated or engraved on order
Weight: 2 pounds, 10 ounces (with 7½" barrel)
Distinctive features: web under barrel cut away; lanyard loop
Markings—
  Top of barrel: REMINGTON ARMS CO., ILION, N. Y.
Serial number: side of grip frame
Dates of manufacture: 1891-1894
Number manufactured: approximately 2,000

Moore

PLATE LVI.
MODEL 51 AUTOMATIC PISTOL
(Semi-automatic)

Markings—
On slide: THE REMINGTON ARMS-UNION METALLIC
CARTRIDGE CO., INC. REMINGTON ILION WKS.
ILION, N.Y. U.S.A. PEDERSEN'S PATENTS PEND-
ING
Serial number: side of frame
Dates of manufacture: 1918-1934
Number manufactured: approximately 65,000

Caliber: .32 A.P.; .380 rimless
Number of shots: 7 in magazine
Barrel: 3½" round (in .380)
Rifling: 7 grooves
Sights: open, Patridge type
Grips: hard rubber, checkered
Finish: dull black
Weight: 1 pound, 6 ounces (in .380)

Moore

PLATE LVII.
MARK III SIGNAL PISTOL

Markings—
Top of barrel: THE REMINGTON ARMS-UNION METALLIC CARTRIDGE CO., INC. MARK III, REMINGTON BRIDGEPORT WORKS BRIDGEPORT, CONNECTICUT, U.S.A.
Dates of manufacture: 1915-1918
Number manufactured: approximately 24,500

Caliber: 10 gauge
Barrel: 9" round, tip-up, steel, dull black
Trigger: sheath
Frame: brass
Grips: walnut, oil finished
Weight: 2 pounds, 7 ounces

7 ▪ ▪

NOTES
FOR THE COLLECTOR

THE THEME AND CONTENT of a collection must, of course, be determined by each individual collector. He alone can decide what arms he desires, what minimum conditions he will accept, and what he can afford. Nevertheless, any completed "specialty" collection of "fine" firearms has a value far greater than the combined values of the individual pieces. Not the least part of that value is the historical significance.

The questions most frequently asked by the average collector concern rarity and price, or rarity versus price. We make no attempt to establish dollar values for any Remington short arms. Varying supply and demand, which determine market prices equally with condition and rarity, would make such a listing of temporary and doubtful worth. The Remington collector does have an advantage in that these arms have been somewhat overlooked until very recent times. Consequently, good pieces have been and still are available in some numbers at moderate prices. Concerning rarity, no one can state positively just how many of any given model of pistol or revolver exists today. A general indication can be obtained from factory production figures and known contracts. The reader may draw his own conclusions from figures and estimates given elsewhere in this book.

The next most important concern of collectors is condition. A surprising number of "fine" to "mint" Remingtons can be found even today. Careful owners, bureau-drawer use, and old dealers' stocks account for the good condition of pocket and belt models. In the case of the service revolvers, one explanation is that many were held in Government arsenals for years and never issued. Arms so held were sold at auction about the turn of the century to firms such as Bannerman. On the other hand, a high percentage of some models saw battle or frontier use. The results are easily imagined: little or no original finish, dents, scratches, mutilated screws, and battered grips. The Beals Army and Navy, the large conversions, and the Frontier are commonly found in this condition. Fine specimens do exist, but are more difficult to find.

A word to the novice may not be out of order. Repaired or refinished arms, particularly the latter, are often a poor buy at any price. If you doubt this, try to sell one to an advanced collector. The average refinished arm is not hard to identify: "heat blue," parkerized type finish, or chromium plate are enough out of character to be recognized easily. Letters and numbers blurred by buffing or plating are also clues to unethical restoration. It is regrettable that this practice has increased in recent years.

Materials. The materials used in the Remington handguns were always the finest available at the time, often in advance of the times. Frames were usually made of wrought iron, but steel, gun bronze, and malleable iron were used on occasion. Barrels and cylinders were normally made only of steel. Trimmings and fittings were iron, gun bronze, or German silver.

Finishes. Remington used whatever finish was in vogue at the particular time. The two most common were charcoal blue and nickel plate. Gold and silver plating was done on special order. A few barrels were finished in hazel brown. A case-hardened frame will be encountered from time to time on the percussion revolvers. Case-hardening was standard on the hammers of percussion service revolvers and on the receivers and trigger guards of martial cartridge single shots. Engraving could be had on any gun at extra charge.

On many of the more decorated revolvers, both large and small, Remington gilded or gold plated the cylinders and silver plated the balance of the gun. In the case of the small pistols, the frames and barrels often differed in finish metal. This two-tone color

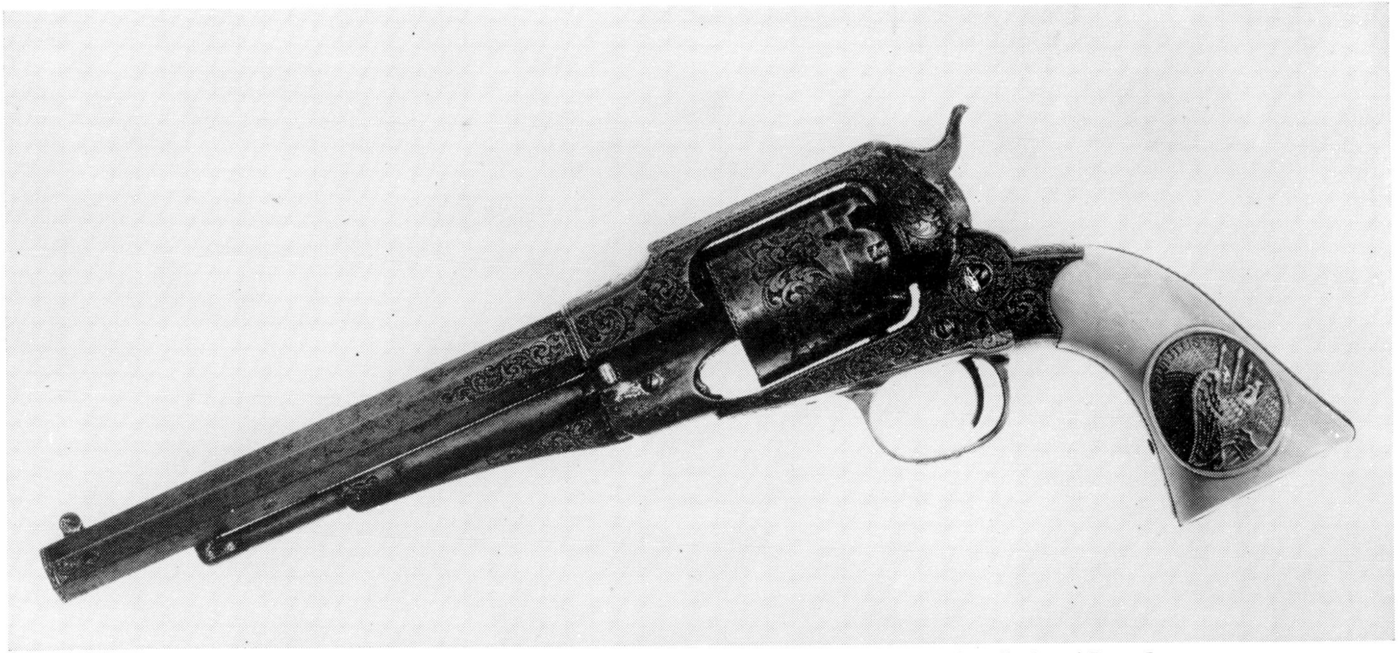

From the collection of Roger Peterson

PLATE LVIII.

scheme was attractive and distinctive since other makers apparently did not use it as much.

Plate LVIII shows a good example of Remington engraving and deluxe ivory grips.

Grips. Remington service arms purchased by the Government on contract after 1862 will have oil finished walnut grips bearing inspectors' initials. If a New Model arm does not have such grips, there is every reason to doubt that it was actually owned by the Government. Model 1861 revolvers, where the practice seems to have started, will be found both with and without the initials. Handguns sold to the general public at the regular list price were equipped with varnished walnut or hard rubber stocks. Pearl, ivory, or rosewood grips could be purchased at varying prices above list.

Markings. All Remington short arms were plainly stamped with the Remington name on either frame or barrel. Specimens found without the Remington name were either stolen from the factory, made by another firm, or made up as pilot models. Serial numbers were usually placed on the underside of the barrel, on the side of the grip frame or on both. Conversion numbers have appeared on the underside of the barrel, the side of the grip frame, the rear of the cylinder, and the side of the frame. Any or all locations may apply to a given piece. Factory custom was, apparently, to stamp either serial or conversion numbers wherever convenient. Inspection numbers or letters have been found just forward of the rammer catch, on the side of the lever rammer, on the side of the barrel, and on the side of the frame. Here again, there was no standard practice. Pistol components were not regularly numbered, but at times this was done to keep fitted parts together. All pistols and revolvers purchased by the Government for actual naval use were stamped with an anchor on the barrel. Most of the so-called "Navys" were actually purchased and issued by the Army.

So many collectors have written in about markings, or rather the lack of them, that a clarification of this subject seems in order.

No written record actually settles one way or another the subject of unmarked guns. However, standard commercial practice of the times left an avenue open for some unmarked guns to go to distributors or large dealers. Salesmen's samples could easily account for another group.

Too, the tremendous volume of material that can escape from an arms factory in the course of five years, let alone fifty, is a point that can not be overemphasized. Casual gifts by management to visitors even can assume importance over a period of years. These and other factors can needlessly confuse the arms student. It was to eliminate as much as possible of the confusion that we listed only standard models in the catalogue sections.

Variations. It would be well to reiterate that Remington did extensive custom gunsmithing. Whatever a customer wanted, within the bounds of sanity, he could have. It is entirely possible that a collector will turn up a gun with almost any sort of variation from standard models. One known specimen of the New Model Navy .36 is anchor stamped, full nickel plated, and ebony gripped. A New Model Army .44 has been seen with a case-hardened frame and a trooper and company number on the right side of the barrel.

MISCELLANEOUS COMMENTS

In tracing the development of minor parts in percussion revolvers, the "single-tined" cylinder bolts in Army and Navy Beals should not be ignored. Later arms were equipped with "double-tined" bolts.

Concerning the changeover from concealed barrel threads to visible ones, Model 1861 Army with serial number 6494 has the Beals type frame; Model 1861 Army with serial number 8342, the later type.

A Model 1865 Navy in the authors' collection has the serial number 143. This low number undoubtedly places it among the original trial pieces. Four of its features are worthy of mention: (a) an 8½″ barrel; (b) the anchor stamped on top of the barrel —the only Government mark; (c) a slab-sided grip with flat bottom, apparently original (pictured in "A New Chapter in an Old Story," Remington, 1912); (d) bearing bosses on the hammer, but none on the breech block.

Readers will note that the contract of November 14, 1866 for 5,000 Navy .50 caliber pistols (later extended to 6,500) has not been listed in Appendix A. The omission is intentional. The published statement of the Remington Company in 1875 that they had furnished the U. S. Navy with 7,000 "old model" pistols, is more comprehensive. The statement is translated as meaning that a grand total of 7,000 Model 1865 and Model 1867 pistols were delivered to the Navy. The discrepancy of 500 arms is easily explained by the known Government practice of using "purchase orders" (not contracts) to obtain small quantities of items for trial. The late 1860's saw service experiments with dozens of arms, a number of which are little known today. Very likely the 500 pistols in question were sold through such an arrangement sometime between April 1866 and early 1867 and were what is known as the Model 1865. What cannot be established with accuracy is the number of this same model, or variations thereof, which may have been delivered in the first stages of the 1866 contract. To assume arbitrarily that the first pistols made on the contract were "pure" Model 1867 is taking entirely too much for granted. The high serial numbers found on some so-called 1865's not only prove the sale of the item to general trade, but also support the growing opinion that the Navy accepted a high number of sheath trigger guns, most of which were recalled and equipped with trigger guards at a later date. In any case, a considerable stock of all parts for both models was still on hand at the Remington factory as late as 1875.

Break-points between percussion models made during the Civil War were established by analysis of patent dates, delivery figures, and official statements of the Remingtons. In this connection, it is well to mention the subject of serial numbers as a clue to total production figures. On .44 percussions, present indications point strongly to the possibility that Remington started with No. 1 on the Beals and continued without a break to the last of the New Models. Highest New Model .44 serial number actually seen to date is 147,283. On .36 percussions, Remington apparently followed the same practice. Highest New Model .36 serial number actually seen to date is 44,943. It is known that the Remington Company started over again at least twice in numbering the Double Derringers. Other Derringer and pocket model numbers should be studied over a period of years to determine the practice followed in their respective cases. A serial number on a Model 1891 Target Pistol gives a possible clue, by inference, to the number of Model 1869 Targets produced. Slightly in excess of 100 Model 1891 Target pistols were made and sold. One specimen bears the serial number 473. If the number is not a hangover from the gun's military past, it might very well indicate, granting that consecutive numbers were used, that no less than 350 Model 1869 Target pistols were made and sold.

Remington collectors will note with interest one item concerning the popularity of these revolvers in Civil War time. "Sale of Arms by United States Government" (1872) records total purchases by returning veterans of 9,875 Remington revolvers, as compared to 9,047 Colts.

As far as can be determined, the Remington Company did not make its own flasks. These were probably purchased from the American Flask and Cap Company, of Waterbury, Connecticut. The American Flask catalog of 1860 shows a Remington type pistol flask; the Remington catalog of 1876 carries a full-page advertisement of that same Connecticut firm. The connection seems obvious.

The pistol flasks cased with the pocket revolvers, such as the Rider or Beals, are the only ones that might be considered as "standard" Remington flasks. The early ones were made of brass; later ones, of copper. They resemble the so-called Colt type: they are 3 3/16″ long not including the spout; the design is a spread eagle holding a shield, surrounded by thirteen stars, with crossed pistols underneath. In some instances, there will be a banner with the raised letters "REMINGTON ILION N. Y." under the crossed pistols.

Flasks cased with the larger revolvers appear to have been whatever Remington had in stock; they follow no standard pattern and do not bear the Remington name.

Remington did manufacture and sell ball-and-bullet, ball, and gang bullet molds, though few were stamped with the firm name.

One collector has a ball-and-bullet pistol mold marked "Remington Ilion N. Y.," the only marked specimen known to us.

Another collector has a single-shot, side lock percussion pistol of the so-called "River Captain" type with a Remington lock. The gun has no other markings.

Plate XXXIII, a reproduction of a factory drawing, illustrates some parts of the Remington "Mexican" Model. We have found no additional data, nor have we examined any complete specimen.

8 ■ ■

NOTES
FOR THE SHOOTER

MOST OF THIS CHAPTER deals with shooting of percussion revolvers. Specific comments on mechanical construction and use are made, of course, with only the Remington handguns in mind.

CHOICE OF ARM

Although it is quite possible to use the early Beals and 1861 model guns, the New Model percussion revolvers are recommended for best results. They were the last to be made and represent the highest development of the cap-and-ball arm. The Army .44 and the Navy, Belt, and Police .36's offer a wide field of choice. Personally, we prefer the .36's because of the lighter powder charge and overall weight. But there are any number of shooters who swear by the .44. Excellent target results can be obtained with either caliber if correctly and carefully loaded.

Use of the New Model Pocket .31 is not encouraged. The short sighting radius handicaps an average marksman, and the stubby lever rammer makes it a little difficult to load.

In choosing an individual arm for shooting, pay particular attention to tightness and structural integrity of the main parts. Make sure there is no wide gap between the cylinder and the breech end of the barrel; excessive pressure loss and flash will result from too great a clearance. Check for cracks and bulges in the cylinder and barrel. Avoid cracked or battered nipples, unless you are positive that they can be removed and replaced. Watch also for nipples with enlarged passages (or vents); too much blowback at this point will scatter pieces of cap and possibly cause double-discharge. Examine the trigger nose and hammer sear notches; if they are chipped or battered, there will be excessive wear and a chance of accidental discharge. Check the operation of hand and bolt; see that the hand rotates the cylinder properly and the bolt locks it in "battery" (chamber lines up with bore). There should be little or no play when the cylinder is locked in place. Do not turn down a good tight arm just because of a few pits in the bore. They will not affect accuracy to any extent, if at all. "Acceptable defects" also include broken or missing hand and sear springs. Such parts break frequently and are replaced often in the course of regular usage.

It is considered short-sighted practice to choose a "fine" to "mint" arm for constant plinking and target shooting. By all rights, the beautiful specimens belong in collections where they will be kept in that condition. Even the most carefully maintained gun will show finish wear, flash-pitting, and scratches after only a moderate amount of range and field use. Since many of the second-rate collection specimens will perform equally as well as those with a lot of original factory finish, use of the former is definitely encouraged.

PREPARATION FOR SHOOTING

First of all, remove the grips and put them aside. Then soak the entire gun, as is, in kerosene for at least twenty-four hours. Although conservative, this procedure will pay dividends. The screws on even a perfect specimen may very well be "frozen" in place with dried grease and a touch of rust.

After the soaking, bring the hammer to half-cock, drop the rammer lever, push forward the cylinder pin, and remove the cylinder to the *right*. Drop the hammer to forward position again.

Now, clean out all the screw slots with a fine pointed instrument; this will allow full purchase for the screwdriver. Using screwdrivers that *fit*, remove the rammer screw, rammer assembly, trigger guard screw, trigger guard, sear spring screw, sear spring, trigger screw, trigger, and bolt, in that order. Next, grasp the piece around the frame and press downward on the top of the hammer; this lessens mainspring pressure on the hammer screw and facilitates its removal. Maintaining pressure on the hammer, move it rearwards a little and let it come up slowly till all mainspring tension is relieved. You may now tap out the mainspring with a brass drift and small hammer. The spring slot is normally tapered, so be sure to drive it out the *large* side. Then, slide the hammer down toward the bottom of the frame to uncover the screw holding the hand in place. Remove this hand screw, then withdraw the hand downward and the hammer upward through the top of the frame. Assembly is accomplished in exactly the reverse order.

Do a thorough job of cleaning the dried grease and rust from all parts, inside and out. If it looks feasible, and it is certainly desirable, remove the nipples from the cylinder and clean all surfaces well, reassembling with a little good grease. Do *not* buff or put parts against a scratch-brush wheel; these practices have ruined more good guns than we care to think about. Patches of rust can be removed very efficiently, with no harm to metal surfaces, by using a small *brass* brush, the edge of a flat brass strip, or fine steel wool.

Check the nipple vents and see that they are clear. If they should not be, a little kerosene, a fine needle, and some lung power will work wonders. The problem of worn down or defective nipples is easily solved when they are removable and can be replaced with new ones. When they are not removable, about the only recourse in combating worn ones is to grind away a little of the forward surface of the hammer body and the inside of the frame at the top. This practice is definitely not recommended, but, if unavoidable, should be done by an expert diemaker or gunsmith.

When all parts have been cleaned, reassemble with a high grade of gun oil.

LOADING

A suitable bullet mold and powder flask are minimum requirements for convenient loading of percussion revolvers. The large six-cavity "armory" molds, with long iron or wooden handles, are excellent but somewhat scarce nowadays. The common pistol ball-and-bullet mold of Civil War days is quite adequate if equipped with wooden extension handles. To operate the contrivance as is, a man would need asbestos hands after casting the first few bullets. Fortunately, extension handles are not difficult to attach, and the device is then usable for a lengthy casting session. Use only soft lead for bullets.

In the past few years we have gone even more extensively into range experimentation with the percussion revolvers. The results, as well as some constantly repeated questions from shooters, merit some comment.

The relatively slow gain twist of Remington barrels propels a round ball with very presentable target results. We recommend the ball, particularly when cast with a modern set of proper mold blocks. A conical bullet, especially the standard Civil War item, is hard to cast, difficult to seat and cranky in performance. We do not mean to belittle the results that can be obtained by the real fanatic using some modern bullet design and precision loading.

A modern mold is definitely preferred equipment for casting. "Vintage" molds wander over a fantastic range of diameters in the same alleged caliber; their most common fault is an oversize egg-shaped product.

Some leeway can be allowed in choosing a powder flask. One with a small charging neck can be used for reduced loads. If the charge thrown is too large, a small ringed plug can be made to hold in the spout while flipping the gate valve.

Number 11 percussion caps are the correct size for the Remington revolvers. New stocks of these are again on the market. Use only *black* or King's Semi-Smokeless powder unless you want to risk being mangled with flying iron. This is the powder the guns were designed for, and it is *all* they will take. FFFg is about right for the .36's and FFg for the .44's, but there is no law against using the same grain for both calibers.

In black powder, a common tendency is the use of too much in too coarse a grain. We now use only 12-14 grains of FFFg in both .36 and .44 and would go to FFFFg if it was more readily obtainable. With proper greasing, a light load is not only consistent but clean shooting.

Before loading, fire a cap on each nipple to clear the vents. Then bring the hammer to half-cock, so that the cylinder is free to rotate. Charge the spout of the flask while holding it upside down with one finger over the nozzle. Pour the charge into one of the chambers, seat the ball or bullet over the chamber mouth, then rotate the cylinder until the ball is under the rammer, and operate the rammer to seat the ball. Repeat this operation for the remaining chambers. No wad or bullet patch is needed; in fact, they are undesirable. The average Civil War period mold in good condition will cast a bullet that is just a good press-fit in the chamber. To avoid having to wipe excess fouling out of the bore after every few shots, it is wise to pack very stiff grease in on top of each ball after the chambers are loaded. When all these operations have been completed, then, and only then, should the caps be placed on the nipples. This safety measure should be observed carefully. Never forget that one of these old guns will kill a man just "as dead" as the most modern firearm. As an added precaution, see that there is no loose powder around the nipples which could cause double-discharge.

SHOOTING

Most of these revolvers will shoot somewhere off the point of aim. A very common tendency is to throw high, particularly if the front sight is worn down a bit. The shooter has two choices: he can "hold off" as a correction, or he can affix a new front sight. If he is a collector and does not want to mar the appearance of the gun, a brass front sight made like a hose-clamp is one solution. The group will also change if the powder charge is varied, as the handloader well knows.

The Remington makes an excellent target revolver. Among its fine points are the solid frame and the quickly removable cylinder. Also, the mass is concentrated in the region of the cylinder, a modern and desirable construction. The shooter will appreciate the wide trigger, the sturdy safety notches on the cylinder shoulders, and the massive, well-designed grips of the Army and Navy models.

CLEANING

As soon after use as possible, clean all the fouled parts with warm water, wipe thoroughly dry, and re-oil. The fouling is corrosive, so haste is imperative.

*   *   *

A number of the conversions and early cartridge Remingtons also provide good shooting sport. Some, but not all, of the different cartridges are still available. You will be wise to make *sure* that the shells are loaded with black powder. The quickest method is to tear a few samples apart. If the bullet grease has dried on, it is well to remove it and re-grease to improve accuracy and cut down fouling. As with the percussion guns, immediate and thorough cleaning after firing is most important.

APPENDIX A

Model and Caliber	Quantity	Customer	Date
Beals .44 (?)	1,000	State of South Carolina	1860
Beals .36	7,350	U. S. Government	8/17/1861 to 3/31/1862
Beals .44	850	U. S. Government	3/31/1862
Model 1861 .44	4,902	U. S. Government	7/12/1862 to 12/31/1862
Model 1861 .36	5,001	U. S. Government	8/11/1862 to 12/22/1862
New Model .44	109,811	U. S. Government	1/5/1863 to 3/23/1865
Model 1865 .50 Model 1867 .50	7,000	U. S. Government	1866 to 5/2/1868
New Model .44	20,000	France	1870
Model 1871 .50	5,000	U. S. Government	1872
Model 1875 .44	10,000	Egypt	1875
Model 1875 .44	6,000(?)	U. S. Government(?)	1875 1876
Mexican Model .38	2,000	Mexico	By 1895

BIBLIOGRAPHY

Norton, Charles B., Brevet Brig. Gen. U.S.V., *American Breech-Loading Small Arms,* New York, 1872

Remington Arms Co., "A New Chapter In An Old Story," 1912

Remington Arms Co., "Centennial Book," 1916

Remington Arms Co., "A Brief History," 1946

Remington, Catalogs and Price Lists, 1857-1910

Russell, Albert N., "Ilion And The Remingtons." An address delivered before the Herkimer County Historical Society, September 14, 1897

Holt-Owen on Ordnance, Senate Ex. Doc. 72, 37th Congress, 2d Session, 1862

Purchase of Ordnance, Executive Document No. 99, 40th Congress, 2d Session, House of Representatives, 1868

Sale of Arms by United States Government, Report No. 183, 42d Congress, 2d Session, May 11, 1872

MODEL INDEX